WATERSIDE PUBS

To the memory of many a canalside pub visit with my wife, Sarah (1943–1997)

WATERSIDE PUBS

The Best Pubs on the Inland Waterways

MIKE LUCAS

Waterways World
Burton-on-Trent

Published by Waterways World Ltd
151 Station Street, Burton-on-Trent,
Staffordshire DE14 1BG, England
Tel: 01283 742950
email: admin@wwonline.co.uk

A catalogue record for this book is available from the British Library

ISBN-13 978 187000209 7

Printed and bound in the United Kingdom by Information Press, Oxford

Opening times: Pub opening times given in this book are correct at the time of writing, but
can change. You are advised to check opening hours before making a long journey.

CONTENTS

KEY MAP TO WATERWAYS

COVERED IN THIS BOOK

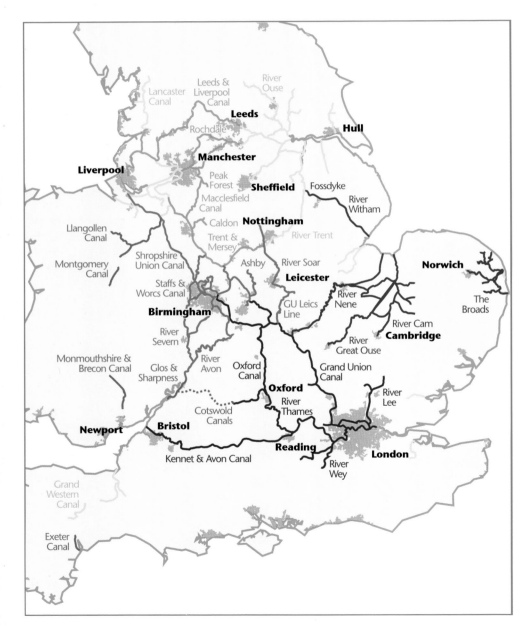

INTRODUCTION

Britain has an amazing system of waterways, consisting of navigable rivers and canals, mainly built in the eighteenth and early nineteenth centuries. This intricate web of water became the new transport link of the emerging Industrial Revolution.

The building of these waterways brought large bands of navigators, or navvies as they became known, to towns and villages along the proposed routes. Inns and pubs opened to slake the thirsts of these men. As the canals were completed and opened, more hostelries were needed to look after the needs of the boat people who were plying their trade, first with boats pulled by horses, later with steamers and motor boats. Many of these pubs survived even after the use of the canals had declined with the arrival of 'better' forms of transport – railways and lorries. Little changed for many years.

After the Second World War and the austerity of the early 1950s, people began to roam further afield to seek their pleasure and relaxation. The motor car enabled them to do this. By the 1960s more and more people were discovering our waterways for walking, fishing and even boating. Three thousand miles of these form a connected system, enabling a boat to travel from Godalming in the south to Ripon in the north of England. A canal holiday was an escape from the realities of everyday living into a peaceful, forgotten world where you were your own boss moving at your own pace. And one of the joys of such holidays was the canalside pub where, if you were lucky, you might share a pint or two with a working boatman. There was still some boat traffic.

I started going on canal holidays with my wife, Sarah, in the mid '60s. We both loved it. So, in 1972, I had a mad idea. I was an actor, a writer and director. Why not form a theatre company that travelled by boat on the waterways taking original theatre to the people? Mikron Theatre Company was born and for the next thirty years I toured with them as we performed in pubs and community halls, on village greens and at boat festivals and rallies.

We all loved our performances in pubs and got to know the landlord and landlady of many of them. We observed the changes as the thirst for real beer from small regional brewers grew, thanks to the influence of the newly-formed Campaign for Real Ale. We gave thanks for the disappearance of the wrinkled ham sandwich and the ever so slightly mouldy pork pie and the emergence of real home-cooked pub grub. We revelled in the fact that there were still canalside pubs where you could play darts and bar billiards, where conversation was not drowned out by the noise of jukeboxes and fruit machines.

But, the rediscovery of the canalside pub came too late for some. They had been demolished to make way for a housing development or a ring road. Others had been extended and modernised in the name of progress or economic necessity. Some, or rather a very few, had remained virtually unaltered, examples of a bygone age. Today these are the jewels in the crown.

In this book you will find a wide variety of canal and riverside pubs. Some are in because they are these jewels in the crown, like the Camp House Inn at Grimley, The Anchor at High Offley, The Boat, Ashleworth Quay, and the Locks Inn, Geldeston. Others are included because of their architecture or their history, like the Bottle & Glass, Dudley and the Olde Black Bear,

Tewkesbury, or their atmosphere or the part they play in the life of a community, like The Boat at Gnosall or The Swan-in-the Rushes, Loughborough. They are all there because they are proper pubs, serving real ales and, often, excellent home-cooked food.

You can visit most of them by car if you wish (you won't get to The Turf Hotel though) but, if you can, go by boat or canoe or walk or cycle along a towpath to them. Whichever way you choose, enjoy them and let the landlord or landlady know that you appreciate that there are still some stunning examples of good pubs along our waterways and that they deserve to be preserved.

Thanks need to go to several people for making the publication of this book possible: Peter Johns, the publisher and managing director at *Waterways World* for having the foresight to spot the relevance of this book; Richard Fairhurst for his wonderful maps and for checking out the details for Other Pubs Worth Trying; Keith Goss for his editing skills and help with Other Pubs Worth Trying; Linda Machin for her design, layout, editing and other tweaking and finally, and certainly not least, to my partner, Lynne, for her help with editing and proof reading and for accompanying me on some of my pub trips and taking some of the photos.

Mike Lucas
2008

CALDER & HEBBLE NAVIGATION
AND ROCHDALE CANAL

Wakefield to Sowerby Bridge: 20 miles/33 locks
Rochdale Canal, Sowerby Bridge to Manchester: 33 miles/92 locks

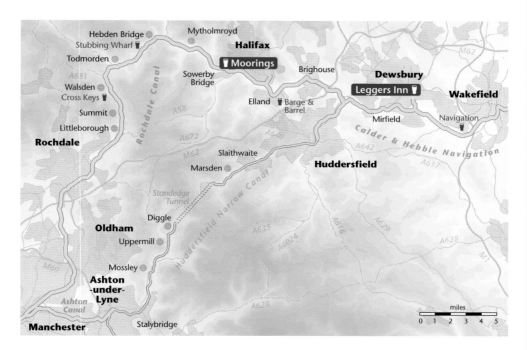

The lower section of the Calder & Hebble between Wakefield and Mirfield has undergone something of a transformation in recent years with many of the surviving mills and warehouses overlooking the waterway converted into up-market flats and apartments. Passing the entrance to the Huddersfield Broad Canal at Coopers Bridge, the canal arrives at Brighouse, which signals the beginning of the most scenic section of the C&H. Through Brookfoot, Cromwell Bottom and Elland, the Calder Valley is at its best: a powerful mix of wooded hillsides and bare rugged hills which industrialisation has only partly compromised. And what a pleasure it is for boaters to cruise on such little used waters – a bit like the pioneering days of the '50s and '60s on the waterways of the Midlands.

At Sowerby Bridge a terminal basin marks the end of the C&H and the junction with the Rochdale Canal.

Rochdale Canal
The reopening of the Rochdale Canal in its entirety in 2002 was a major triumph for the restorationists and opened up many miles of exciting cruising in the North West of England. It is a grand canal, striding manfully along the Calder Valley, up over the Pennines and down into Manchester.

For pubs on the Huddersfield Narrow Canal, see page 13.

THE MOORINGS

Sowerby Bridge, West Yorkshire

PUB FACTS

Location   Canal Wharf, Sowerby Bridge, West Yorks HX6 2AG

Tel   01422 833940

Email   moorings99@btopenworld.com

Website   www.themooringspub.co.uk

Manager   Anthony Parker

Opening hours   Sun–Thu 12pm–11pm, Fri/Sat 12pm–12pm

Food served   Mon–Fri 12pm–2.30pm, 6pm–9pm, Sat 12pm–9pm, Sun 12pm–6pm

Real ales   Black Sheep Best Bitter, Timothy Taylor's Landlord, Ruddles County plus two guest beers, eg London Pride, Theakston's Black Bull Bitter, Greene King IPA

Moorings   Towpath side alongside basin

The Rochdale Canal is a typical trans-Pennine waterway, heavily locked but with bags of magnificent hill scenery as recompense. It runs from Manchester through 92 locks to Sowerby Bridge, 33 miles away in Yorkshire, where it connects with the Calder & Hebble Navigation. You approach Sowerby Bridge Wharf through Tuel Lock, which is fairly daunting with a drop of 20 feet, the deepest on the canal system.

The Calder & Hebble never closed. Opened in 1770, it was a busy commercial waterway until the 1950s, the traffic including sea-going barges between the Humber and the Mersey.

Sowerby Bridge Wharf is magnificent. It is the area around the basin at the head of the Calder & Hebble and is bounded on the south by the Rochdale Canal. A number of grand warehouses were built to service the two canal companies, including the Salt Warehouse for storing salt that had arrived from Cheshire. This and No 4 Warehouse were built with a canal arm inside forming an interior dock for loading and unloading sheltered from the elements.

Over the years, many of these warehouses were allowed to become semi-derelict and at one stage it looked as if this whole cluster of buildings might be lost. But the word 'heritage' became buzzy just in time and a partnership was formed to restore the wharf under the title, 'Regeneration through Heritage'.

Before all this began to happen, No 2 Warehouse had been restored and someone had the bright idea to turn part of it into a pub, the Moorings. And an excellent place it is. An ideal spot to refresh your inner parts after boating down the Rochdale or even, but less deserved, if you're visiting the wharf by car.

There's a large main bar with lots of bench seats and wooden beams which are supported by the original iron stanchions of the warehouse and paintings and mirrors decorate the walls. Tall windows look out on to the basin with its boats, the original wharf manager's office, the back of the Sunday School, Bottom Brow Chapel and

the Assemby Hall, with a distant view of the awesome Wainhouse Tower.

Another smaller room and a dining room complete the pub, apart from the area outside the front, which, on a summer's day, can accommodate a hundred people. Look out for the impressive Lock Keeper and Boy statue.

The Moorings has an excellent choice of real ales including one of my favourites, Black Sheep Best Bitter. The food is also good here. It's all cooked on the premises from fresh ingredients by the three resident chefs. Start with, for example, moules mariniere (£5.75), continue with classic cassoulet (£8.25) and finish with one of their yummy puddings. There's also plenty of choice of hot and cold sandwiches and jacket potatoes.

Sowerby Bridge has come a long way from its Norse origins, 'farmstead on sour ground'. Being at the confluence of the Calder and Ryburn rivers has meant it has been an important crossing point since the Middle Ages. The mills and factories that sprung up during the Industrial Revolution were wonderfully served by the Rochdale Canal and the Calder & Hebble and their superlative wharf. Go and see, drink and eat and enjoy.

THE LEGGERS INN

Dewsbury, West Yorkshire

PUB FACTS

Location	Robinson's Boatyard, Savile Town Wharf, Mill Street East, Dewsbury, West Yorks WF12 9BD
Tel	01924 502846
Owner	Graham Marsh
Manager	John Smithson
Opening hours	Sun–Thu 10.30am–11pm, Fri/Sat 10.30am–12pm
Food served	11am–10pm
Real ales	Everards' Tiger Best Bitter and beers from Rooster's of Knaresborough, eg. Yankee & Cream, plus guests and foreign bottled beers
Moorings	On the arm near to the basin

Dewsbury is an important town. Part of the Heavy Woollen District of West Yorkshire, it is famous for its blankets, flushings, shoddy and mungo.

The Leggers Inn is situated in Savile Town Basin, which lies at the end of what is left of a loop off the main navigation – about three quarters of a mile. The main navigation is the Calder & Hebble which runs 21 miles from the Aire & Calder at Wakefield to Sowerby Bridge.

The Navigation is a mixture of river and short canal sections and also connects with the Huddersfield Broad Canal at Cooper Bridge. Sometimes the river can get quite lively, making for an interesting trip!

Savile Town Basin once had many warehouses and other canal-related buildings. Now all that's left is a little row of terraced houses and the complex in the corner of the basin that houses the offices of Calder Valley Marine, who run the boatyard, the Old Stables Coffee

steak or Cornish pies (made with a 'secret' recipe, Boddingtons beer) and peas, curries, soups, hot dogs and sandwiches.

And that's what sums up the place. It's a proper, old-fashioned friendly pub with an interesting mix of customers: there are workers from the large number of businesses nearby, particularly at lunchtime and in the early evening, and boaters, walkers, bikers (the pub is on the 'Greenway' cycle track) and real ale enthusiasts who come from as far away as London and Liverpool. And, as soon as the weather is decent (well, decent enough for Yorkshire folk, anyway), the tables outside surrounding the basin are chock-a-block.

My advice is to arrive there not only with a thirst but with a problem. At the bar you will probably find a builder, a plumber, an electrician, a lawyer or an accountant. They'll soon sort you out.

Shop and the Leggers Inn. The building used to be stables and a blacksmith's shop.

The pub is on the first floor in the area that was the hayloft for the stables. The large main bar, with views over the basin, is split into two sections: one has a pool table, television (for watching football, of course) and darts board; the other, where the bar is with its decorations of roses and castles, has a colourful variety of sofas and chairs, a motley collection of objects including a cog wheel from a rag mill in Batley, teapots, crates, bottles, a framed jigsaw and lots of pictures. It also boasts a terrific stove that, using coal or wood, provides all the heat.

The Leggers also has a large function room. This is decorated with all manner of signs, including 'Central Criminal Court' under the bar, which are props recycled from television programmes.

The variety of beer is amazing. Apart from the Everards' and Rooster's regulars, you will find the likes of Archer's Headbanger, Tom Wood's Old Timber or Exmoor Gold. The locals go on regular trips to Belgium. Hence the mind-boggling selection of Belgian beers like Duvel, Belle-vue Kriek and Westmalle Trappist.

Food is good simple fare: pork,

OTHER PUBS WORTH TRYING

Calder & Hebble Navigation
and Rochdale Canal

BARGE & BARREL

Elland, West Yorkshire

Park Road, Elland, West Yorkshire
HX5 9HP.
Tel: 01422 373623

(Calder & Hebble)

Here's one for the real ale enthusiast, with
blackboards in front of the bar listing the ales
on offer – as many as 13 on occasions. Some
are brewed on site by the Elland Brewery.
Entertainment is of the pool table, dart board,
jukebox variety and food is available most
lunchtimes and evenings.

NAVIGATION

Calder Grove, Wakefield, West Yorkshire

Broad Cut Road, Calder Grove,
Wakefield, West Yorkshire WF4 3DS
Tel: 01924 274361

(Calder & Hebble)

This family-friendly pub positively exudes
Northern hospitality. The garden is exceptionally
nice and moorings are available. Food is served
lunchtimes throughout the year, evenings too in
summer. Why not call on a Wednesday, the quiz
night, when the winner's prize is a gallon of beer?

STUBBING WHARF

Hebden Bridge, West Yorkshire

King Street, Hebden Bridge,
West Yorkshire HX7 6LU
Tel: 01422 844107
www.stubbingwharf.com

(Rochdale Canal)

Nestling between the Rochdale Canal and the
River Calder, this spacious, welcoming pub offers
a wide range of real ales and hosts a cider festival
in June. Regular entertainment is laid on, including
a 'Shaggy Dog Story' evening.

CROSS KEYS

Walsden, Lancashire

649 Rochdale Road, Walsden,
Todmorden OL14 6SX
Tel: 01706 815185

(Rochdale Canal)

This is 'real pub' country, and the Cross Keys,
above Travis Mill Lock, is a splendid example
of the breed. The ales are served perfectly, the
servings of food are nothing if not generous, and
the staff are friendly; there are moorings, too, and
a conservatory looking onto the canal. And for
true Northern grit, how about this: it was founded
by a family of clog-makers and was once called
the Cloggers Arms.

CALDON CANAL

Etruria to Froghall
17 miles/17 locks/1 tunnel
Leek Branch: 3 miles/1 tunnel

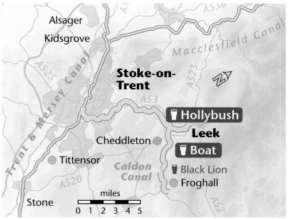

You wouldn't really expect a canal that begins in Stoke-on-Trent to be among the most beautiful in the land, but the Caldon rises manfully to the challenge. In reality it effects its escape from the Potteries (where it joins the Trent & Mersey) remarkably quickly and thereafter revels in glorious moorland scenery all the way to its twin termini at Froghall and at Leek.

Hazelhurst Junction is an exceptionally pretty canal junction, a divine location deep in the Staffordshire Moorlands enhanced by the attendant lock flight and aqueduct. Here the Leek Branch heads off towards that worthy town but the present day terminus lies a few hundred yards short, necessitating completion of the journey on shanks's pony.

The main line continues through the Churnet Valley, traversing increasingly wild and gorgeous countryside, the wooded slopes hereabouts being of almost Amazonian density. Beyond Cheddleton and Consall Forge (linked by a preserved steam railway), the canal eventually terminates at Froghall Wharf, from where horsedrawn trip boats operate on summer weekends. Froghall has been the scene of feverish activity in recent times, as work has been undertaken to restore the top basin and first lock of the linking Uttoxeter Canal.

For the Trent & Mersey Canal, see page 31.

At Hazelhurst Junction the towpath bridge crosses the top lock of the Froghall line to reach the Leek Arm on the right.

BOAT INN

Cheddleton, near Leek, Staffordshire

PUB FACTS

Location	170 Basford Bridge Lane, Cheddleton, near Leek, Staffordshire ST13 7EQ
Tel	01538 360683
Lessee	Edward Christopher Massey
Opening hours	Sun–Thurs 12pm–11pm, Fri & Sat 12pm–12am
Food served	Mon–Sat 12pm–2.30pm, 6pm–9pm, Sun 12pm–4pm (Sunday roast), 4.30pm–9pm (normal menu)
Real ales	Marston's Burton Bitter & Pedigree plus guest beers changing monthly, eg Fine Fettle, Sweet Chariot, Captain Smith
Moorings	Opposite the pub on towpath side

The Boat Inn is located a little out of the village of Cheddleton at Basford Bridge, nestling above the canal. It's a beautiful, long low building made of stone with pretty small-paned windows. If you're arriving by boat or even parking in the car park on the other side of the bridge, it's difficult to appreciate how attractive it is, because the canalside patio has a green canopy over it, obscuring the view. But walk up to the pub and you'll see what I mean. When you go in, you'll get a really friendly welcome from the landlord, Chris. The locals appreciate visitors as well: "We had a group off a boat in and they brought guitars and other instruments. They had a sing-song and impressed the regulars," says Chris.

The Boat Inn is a pub that manages to look after locals and visitors alike, and to cater for people who just want to quaff some good beer and those who want a proper meal. Most of the food is locally sourced and home-made, but Chris did point out that they didn't catch their own scampi. Has he thought of crayfish from the Caldon, I wonder?

The good people of Cheddleton support the pub and Chris supports them. Every November, they hold an auction for charity. There are two darts teams and Sunday quizzes in winter. If you're there in the summer, you may well catch the live music and barbeque on the canalside terrace.

If you're on a boat, continue down the Caldon. It is one of the most picturesque sections on the waterways. The canal locks down into the River Churnet and proceeds via a series of tortuous bends to Consall Forge, set in a steep wooded valley, before becoming a canal again for the trip through the woods to Froghall and its tunnel and basin.

But don't leave without visiting Cheddleton Flint Mill, in Cheddleton itself, and the Churnet Valley Railway across the river from the pub. Flints used to be brought by boat from Kent, loaded into kilns to be burnt for several days. They were then ground and crushed in the water-powered mill and the powder taken by boat to the Potteries to be used to strengthen the clay pots. When the mill closed, it was turned into a museum and provides a magnificent working example of our industrial heritage.

The Pugin railway station is now used by the Churnet Valley Railway. They run steam trains from Leek Brook to Froghall – what a wonderful use of a disused freight line. Go on a trip one-way and walk back along the towpath. You will have worked up a thirst which will necessitate another visit to the Boat Inn.

Cheddleton Flint Mill.

THE HOLLYBUSH INN

Denford, near Leek, Staffordshire

PUB FACTS

Location   Denford Road, Denford,
near Leek, Staffordshire
ST13 7JT

Tel   01538 371819

Proprietor   Dave Coward

Opening hours   Mon–Sat 11am–11pm,
Sun 12pm–10.30pm

Food served   12pm–9pm

Real ales   Fuller's London Pride,
Courage Directors Bitter,
Ruddles County plus guest
beers

Moorings   Outside pub

Nineteen seventy four was a momentous year for the waterways. It was the year of openings; that is, of canals and rivers that had been allowed to fall into dereliction and had now been restored, using both voluntary and professional labour. 1974 saw the re-opening of the Upper Avon, the Peak Forest, the Ashton and the Caldon Canals.

These waterways have a lot to offer and, in the '70s, they all provided a challenge to Mikron as we tried to navigate these 'not quite finished' routes. But the Caldon immediately became one of my favourites, particularly in the early days of its re-opening when it was still 'a secret canal' – the journey through industrial Hanley seemed to deter a lot of boaters. Little did they know what delights would have been in store if they had ventured further. Today, the secret is out but it's still a journey worth making.

Not least for its canalside pubs. There are several gems and the Hollybush Inn is definitely one of them. It stands on the canalside, but it is only a hundred yards from the back of the pub to the Leek Arm, which has departed from the main line at Hazelhurst Junction and passed over it via Hazlehurst Aqueduct, again near to the Hollybush.

This remarkable piece of engineering was completed in 1841. At that time there was a flour mill on the site of the pub, using water from Endon Brook. At some point before 1885, the engine house of the mill was turned into an inn. The mill itself survived into the 20th century when it was replaced by a row of cottages.

The pub still retains the intimate, friendly atmosphere I first encountered in the mid-seventies. The very large holly bush, which gave the pub its name, has gone to make way for a conservatory; the old stable is now a bar and new additions include a restaurant, a rear bar and a garden, and a large children's play area out the back, where the youngsters can jump and climb to their hearts' content and mingle with the goats, chickens and rabbits.

But the front of the pub is unchanged and so is the original bar. Open the sliding doors to gain entry. Pause to look at the books on sale as you walk to the bar. Buy yourself a pint. Then go and sit by the blazing log fire (not in summer, obviously - sit outside by the canal instead and watch the boaters having some difficulty negotiating the tricky bends). Order some of the delicious home-cooked food (bar meals at lunch time from sandwiches and baguettes to their famous Beef in Beer Casserole, with more choice in the evening including steaks, curries and the daunting Hollybush Country Grill with lamb, pork, gammon, steak, sausages, onions, mushrooms and egg).

There are many reasons to visit the Hollybush – the canals, the scenery, the beer, the food and the atmosphere. You can no longer play Bar Skittles (sadly, the skittles and, even, the chain and ball kept being stolen - a sad reflection on our times), but you can talk. There's no jukebox or telly. And you can take your beloved dog with you. There are sometimes more dogs than people and they're much better behaved! On the day I was there, pub customers included a Husky and a Jack Russell, and that was a winter lunchtime. It must be like Crufts in the summer!

OTHER PUBS WORTH TRYING

Caldon Canal

BLACK LION

Consall Forge, Stoke-on-Trent
Consall Forge, Wetley Rocks,
Stoke-on-Trent ST9 0AJ
Tel: 01782 550294

A priceless gem – a pub with limited access by road (in fact a deeply rutted track). Most patrons come by boat (good moorings opposite), by preserved steam railway or on foot from Cheddleton or Froghall to find this totally unspoilt hostelry. There's a good range of real ales, food at lunchtimes and evenings and wonderful views of the remote and beautiful Churnet Valley.

HUDDERSFIELD NARROW CANAL

Huddersfield to Dukinfield Junction
20 miles/74 locks/3 tunnels

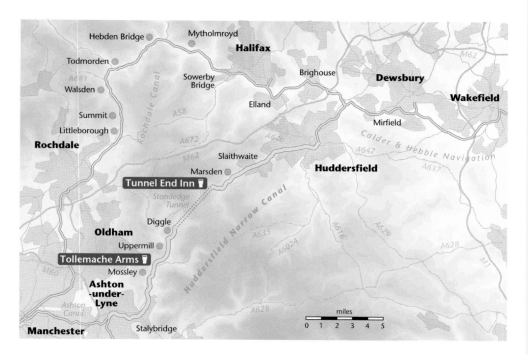

The reopening of the Huddersfield Narrow Canal in 2001 was the cause of celebration in waterway circles, being the culmination of almost 30 years of campaigning and restoration work. Notwithstanding all the euphoria, the canal has yet to achieve a high level of popularity with many boaters; 74 locks within the space of 20 miles and Pennine scenery compromised by industrial scars, past and present, may be responsible. Nevertheless, it is pleasing to be able to report that boater numbers continue to increase, so the future looks bright for the HNC.

From Aspley Basin, the canal climbs relentlessly up to the summit at Marsden. For many visitors, Standedge Tunnel – the longest (at 3 miles 418 yards), deepest and highest canal tunnel in Britain – represents the highlight of the Huddersfield Narrow.

Thereafter, it's all downhill for the HNC, as it descends through Diggle, Mossley and Stalybridge to Ashton-under-Lyne, where the canal effects an end on junction with the Ashton Canal. This couldn't be described as the prettiest section of canal in the world, but don't despise it on that account; industrial archaeologists will find a wealth of interest and the wonderful achievement of the restorationists – not least in the vicinity of Stalybridge where innumerable barriers and difficulties were overcome – should never be forgotten. For a variety of reasons, the HNC belongs on the true canal enthusiasts must see list.

For pubs on the Calder & Hebble Navigation and Rochdale Canal, see page 1.

TOLLEMACHE ARMS

Mossley, Greater Manchester

PUB FACTS

Location	415 Manchester Road, Mossley, Greater Manchester OL5 9BG
Lessee	Diane Harrison
Opening hours	Sun–Thu 12pm–12am, Fri/Sat 12pm–1am
Real ales	Robinson's Old Stockport and Unicorn
Moorings	Towpath side outside pub

The Tollemache Arms is a perfect canalside local in the old tradition – no frills or fripperies, a friendly, welcoming alehouse. It is a pub that has regulars, some of whom have been going there since time immemorial. There's a darts team, a crib team and a quiz team. There's a cricket team in the summer and the Tollemache Golf Association meets there (not to play golf, I'm assured). There's a sign on the wall that says: "When primitive man screamed and beat the ground with sticks, they called it witchcraft. Modern man calls it golf." The eggman comes round on a Friday and, if you want a plumber or a brickie, just ask.

They come to drink the excellent Robinson's beer, to talk and sometimes watch football on Sky Sports. Occasionally, there'll be live music or a race night. But do they welcome boaters? "Flipping 'eck, of course we do, " says Diane, the landlady. "And walkers. Last weekend, we had twenty cyclists stop off."

The land that the pub is on was originally owned by the Tollemache family. Three dwelling houses were built by John Roach in 1837, when a new turnpike opened to Greenfield. These were converted into a public house somewhere between 1847 and 1866. It became a Robinson's pub in 1926.

When you walk into 'The Tolly', you'll immediately feel at home. There's a main room with a lovely wooden bar and pictures of the pub and the canal on the wall, and an even smaller snug for those who want more intimate conversations. There's no food but why not try a packet of pork scratchings – real ones from the Black Country. If you're there in the winter, warm your parts with a half of Old Tom straight from the barrel. No more, mind. It's 8.5%.

And then go for a walk around Mossley. It's a small town full of character with stone houses built on the steep streets. Wandering about, you'll spot many weavers' cottages, with the weaving room on the top storey, and textile mills, many of these now used for all sorts of purposes but weaving.

On the hillside above is Buckton Castle, an Iron Age hill fort. You can still see the defensive ridge and ditch. Running across the fields below is an ancient road. The Romans saw how useful this could be, paved it and used it as a route between two of their camps, Melandra (Glossop) and Castleshaw (Saddleworth).

Dropping back down to the canal (a vital new trans-Pennine link when first opened in 1811), call in for another pint at the Tolly, impress the locals with your knowledge of the area – but only talk about football if you support Manchester United!

TUNNEL END INN

Marsden, Huddersfield, West Yorkshire

The hard work of boating up and down the Pennines along the restored Huddersfield Narrow Canal is more then compensated for by the harsh but dramatic scenery, the friendly villages and towns and the trip through the tunnel. But whether you are on a boat, walking, cycling, visiting by train (Marsden Station is just down the road) or even in a car, you must not go to the Marsden end of the tunnel without visiting the Tunnel End Inn, a hundred yards up the hill, leading away from the very grand British Waterways warehouse.

The Tunnel End Inn (or Junction Hotel as it was called until 1989) was built as a pub at about the same time as the canal. It was used by local farmers and boatpeople and must have been a very welcome haven on the occasional cold, windy night you get in this part of the world.

It still is a haven for regulars and visitors alike. Bev and Gary bought the pub in 2002.

They have changed it very little. It's intimate, full of character with a huge log fire in the main bar, a snug and a small restaurant.

Everyone is made very welcome and personally attended to by the landlords. As Bev says: "I love mystery shoppers. You never know who they might be." She was delighted when David Trimble wandered in. He was on a boat holiday. Gary treats his beers with care and affection. The Black Sheep and Landlord are always worth quaffing but be adventurous and try his guest beers. You might get Golden Glow from Dudley, Angel Hill from Boggart Hole Clough, Copper Dragon from Skipton or Holme Valley Special from Holmfirth.

The food's good too. "We're not a restaurant," says Bev, "but a pub serving proper home-made meals." Try the steak and ale pie, the chicken and leek pie or broccoli and brie rosti. And there's always a traditional roast on Sundays and Bank Holidays.

The locals support the pub with their darts and quiz teams, and there are often special quiz nights or 'open mic' evenings in aid of charity. If you're a visitor, you just join in.

Lots of walkers call in at the pub, and who can blame them after a hard slog over Standedge Hill, but Bev would like to see more people from the canal. She often goes down to the tunnel with her dog, and chats to boaters and invites them to call in and relax for an hour or so. She will always cook especially for you, outside of official food hours, if you just let her know you're coming.

The Huddersfield Narrow is a beautiful canal. Some of its stretches are unrivalled in the country and the area around the tunnel is particularly dramatic. So, head up north and straight to its delights and those of the Tunnel End Inn.

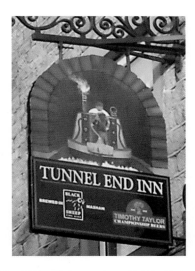

PUB FACTS

Location	Waters Road, Marsden, Huddersfield, West Yorkshire HD7 6NF
Tel	01484 844636
Email	info@tunnelendinn.com
Website	www.tunnelendinn.com
Proprietors	Bev & Gary Earnshaw
Opening hours	Mon 8pm–11pm, Tue–Thu 5pm–11pm, Fri–Sun 12pm–11pm
Food served	Wed 6pm–9pm (home-made pie & peas), Fri 12pm–2.30pm, 6pm–8pm, Sat 12pm–3.30pm, 6pm–8pm, Sun 12pm–4pm
Real ales	Timothy Taylor's Landlord, Black Sheep Best Bitter and two changing guest beers
Moorings	Outside Standedge Tunnel
Rooms	Self-contained flat, sleeps four

Bingley Five Rise Locks on the Leeds & Liverpool Canal.

LEEDS & LIVERPOOL CANAL

Leeds to Liverpool
127 miles/93 locks/2 tunnels
Leigh Branch: 7 miles/2 locks. Rufford Branch: 7 miles/8 locks

The Leeds & Liverpool is, in football manager's parlance, a canal of two halves. The eastern section is simply glorious, standing comparison with any canal in the land; west of Foulridge Tunnel the L&L is less scenic, as it passes through a succession of industrial Lancashire towns before terminating in Liverpool's somewhat intimidating docklands. Nevertheless, for those of sufficient fortitude this represents one of the great canal voyages, a magnificent coast-to-coast journey across northern England.

Escaping swiftly from the urban environs of Leeds, the canal climbs out of the Aire Valley through a series of locks, climaxing in the famous Bingley Five Rise flight. Numerous swing bridges provide plenty of additional exercise and the surroundings are never less than pleasant. Indeed, Saltaire – home of Sir Titus Salt's model workers' village – is a truly magical location.

The finest section of the canal begins at Skipton. For the next 15 miles or so it carves its way through exquisite Pennine scenery – a wild landscape of stone farms and cottages with wide-ranging views to all points of the compass. This is walker's country, too, and indeed the Pennine Way crosses the waterway at East Marton.

The party's over once you reach Foulridge Tunnel, by now ensconced in Lancashire. Nelson, Burnley and Blackburn greet the northbound canal traveller. Then comes Wigan, perhaps best known for its George Orwell connections and its rugby league and football clubs, where boaters often tackle the flight of 21 locks in convoy to deter hooligans. Thereafter, the canal finds sanctuary in the wooded valley of the River Douglas, before arriving at the attractive village of Parbold.

It's not long before Liverpool's outer suburbs begin to appear on the horizon. Few boaters venture beyond Aintree, home of the world famous Grand National steeplechase. Henceforth the canal is 'remaindered', although passage to the docklands terminus can be arranged through British Waterways' North West office.

The Leigh Branch runs from Wigan to Leigh where it joins the Bridgewater Canal. The Rufford Branch leads from Burscough to the River Douglas, an extremely beautiful waterway – almost Fenlandesque in character – which now provides access to the Lancaster Canal via the Ribble Link.

THE ANCHOR INN

Salterforth, Barnoldswick, Lancashire

PUB FACTS

Location	Salterforth Lane, Salterforth, Barnoldswick, Lancashire BB18 5TT
Tel	01282 813186
Lessee	Michael Metcalfe
Opening hours	Sun–Thu 12pm–11pm, Fri/Sat 12pm–12.30am
Food served	Mon–Fri 12pm–2pm, 5.30pm–9pm, Sat 12pm–9pm, Sun 12pm–8pm (Main dishes from £5.25–£11)
Real ales	Deuchars IPA, Courage Directors Bitter, John Smith's Bitter plus two changing guest beers
Moorings	Outside pub on towpath side

Imagine the scene: you are a traveller arriving in Salterforth in any year between 1655 and 1788. You are a drover with your beasts on the way to market, or a salter carrying your precious cargo of salt from Cheshire to Whitby. Suddenly, you are plummeted forward in time to the 21st century. At first, everything appears normal. But what you knew as Salters Ford is now Salterforth. The stables for your mules seem to have disappeared. The pub has changed its name and grown a storey, and there is a ribbon of waterway running past outside.

But the remarkable thing is that, if the traveller looked closer, he would still find his beloved Traveller's Rest, which makes this pub one of the most fascinating I have ever visited.

It's the oldest building left standing in

Salterforth. Built in 1655, it was an important stopping point on the packhorse route into Yorkshire. It survived unchanged until the excavation of the Leeds & Liverpool Canal in 1778. The pub was beneath the waterline of the new waterway and became impossibly damp. So, the simple solution was to build a new pub on top of the old. The rooms where the drovers would have sat in front of fires and been revived with ale brought to them in a jug became the cellars, and the bedrooms above became the new bars. Another storey was built for sleeping.

The Canal Tavern (as it was appropriately renamed) now serviced quarrymen, stone wallers, canal labourers and boatmen. Mysteriously, it changed its name to the Anchor Inn in about 1900 (is there something about navigating the Leeds & Liverpool I don't know about?).

The building outside remains unaltered to this day. But what would amaze the drover and the salter is their old Traveller's Rest. The rooms are still there, albeit with barrels of beer and other cellar impedimenta. The original oak front door is still there. Open that, and you step out from the original entrance on to the old packhorse road. It has been covered with an arch to take pressure off the pub from the canal bank. Over the years, the

water leaking from the canal has carried the limestone out of the mortar and beautiful, thin and delicate stalactites and stalagmites have been formed. Some of them are so long that they are now touching in the middle.

Ask if you can visit the cellars and step back in history. Listen out for the voices of the travellers of yesterday. But be careful where you stand and do not be tempted to touch - unlike the celebrants on VE night in 1945. There is still a blank spot where they got carried away by the excitement of the hour.

The Anchor Inn is well worth visiting for other reasons – a friendly atmosphere, good real ales and delicious home-cooked food. All the food is made on the premises by the two chefs, and the meat and veg are all sourced locally. There are always home-made pies and curry of the week. The pub has a good local trade, although the setting, the food and the beer attract people from far afield.

On a summer's day, there'll be bikes propped alongside the pub, children playing on the swings in the garden, and people draped on the bridge watching the hire boats negotiate the daunting 90° turn. Terrible muddles can ensue, followed by flailing poles and rising tempers. All great fun for the gongoozlers above.

THE NAVIGATION

Blackburn, Lancashire

PUB FACTS

Location	2 Canal Street, Mill Hill, Blackburn, Lancashire BB2 4DL
Tel	01254 53230
Lessee	Barbara Hickey
Opening hours	Mon–Sat 10.30am–12.30am, Sun 11am–12pm
Food served	Crisps and nuts only
Real ales	Thwaites' Original Bitter & Dark Mild
Moorings	Alongside towpath outside pub

Barbara Hickey has been the landlady at the Navigation for 28 years, the longest-serving publican in the Blackburn district. She runs a down-to-earth local. It was built at about the same time as the canal. The Leeds & Liverpool was finally opened throughout its length in 1816. At 127 miles, it is the longest continuous canal in Britain built by a single company.

The Navigation would have serviced the boatpeople and provided stabling for their horses. The stables are still there today, sadly no longer in use. The last occasion was when Barbara's daughter kept her horse there: "We thought it were just fat but it turned out to be pregnant. So we ended up with two."

The pub overlooks the canal, with a cobbled slope running down from the road above. Two benches, ingeniously attached to the pub wall, provide a spot for boat watching. Inside, there have been some structural changes. In 1975, the small rooms were very sympathetically converted into two large ones: the Vault, where you can watch telly or play darts and dominoes, and the Music Room, where there is a pool table and juke-box and where, if you're lucky, you'll catch the regulars singing and dancing to '60s music.

It's the sort of pub that people remember from their childhood. One woman came back from Canada on a visit. She remembered sledging down the hill and straight through the door of the pub, where she was greeted by her dad: "What art thou doing 'ere, lass?" Another woman turned up and said she had been born in the pub and that, when she was a baby, her cot had been a drawer in the bar. Many memories. "Everything creaks", says Barbara.

Visitors are warmly welcomed and soon enveloped in the bar banter. The beer is delicious and cheap. Give the dark mild a go. Very few pubs sell it and the Navigation has a reputation for this malty, caramel brew. Visiting football fans call in for a pint, before wandering along the towpath to Ewood Park, the home of Blackburn Rovers.

Blackburn itself is well worth a visit. The town began to flourish during the Industrial Revolution. Its climate was ideal for cotton spinning and weaving. Inventors like John Kay, James Hargreaves and Richard Arkwright patented machines which took people away from their homes and into the new factory system. Home-produced Blackburn linen checks were replaced by cotton goods, especially calicoes.

Some of the old cotton mills are still there and textiles are still being produced. But for a glimpse of the past, try the Lewis Textile Museum, where the many full-sized working models include Blackburn's very own James Hargreaves' Spinning Jenny.

Excise officer, Daniel Thwaites, founded Thwaites' Star Brewery in Blackburn in 1807. It remains independent and is one of the oldest family-run Lancashire firms, with a beer museum you can visit.

But the main reason for your trip has to be the Navigation. Barbara says that last year there were quite a few boats on the canal, but not many stopped outside her pub, though "they do wave". Well, don't wave. Tie up for the evening and relax in a proper pub. It's a good safe mooring and feels quite rural. At the last count, there were 50 ducks, 30 Canada geese, two swans plus cygnets and several moorhens. Back to Barbara: "Glory be. Look at all this in the middle of Blackburn. I love it here. I've never wanted to move."

OTHER PUBS WORTH TRYING

Leeds & Liverpool Canal

LATHOM SLIPWAY

Burscough, Lancashire
48 Crabtree Lane, Burscough,
Lancashire L40 0RN
Tel: 01704 897767.

A children-friendly garden (climbing frames, trikes and more), Thwaites ale, hearty food, and you can watch boaters struggle with the swing-bridge – what more could you ask for in a canalside pub? This former CAMRA Summer Pub of the Year has thoroughly earned its good reputation with both locals and canal travellers alike.

THE ALBION

Clayton-le-Moors, Lancashire
243 Whalley Road, Clayton-le-moors,
Accrington, Lancashire BB5 5HD
Tel: 01254 2384585

Clayton-le-Moors is arguably one of the less attractive towns along the entire length of the Leeds & Liverpool Canal; it's all the more surprising, then, to encounter this excellent pub beside Bridge 114A. A fine selection of real ales and cider, good home cooked food, plentiful moorings and occasional evening entertainment are among the attractions on offer.

INN ON THE WHARF

Burnley, Lancashire
Manchester Road, Burnley, Lancashire
BB11 1JG
Tel: 01282 459951

Located in a former weaver's warehouse – all original beams, flagstone floors etc – this smart pub caters for young professionals, families and boaters. There's a good range of real ales, and food is available lunchtimes and evenings – anything from bar snacks to full à la carte. Canalside seating is provided and there are moorings for visiting boaters.

NARROW BOAT

Skipton, West Yorkshire
38 Victoria Street, Skipton,
West Yorkshire BD23 1JE
Tel: 01756 797922

A former wine bar, this is a real ale drinker's paradise with a huge and rotating choice of beers. The food's good too and there is a nice outside seating area by the canal. There's no piped music – you can actually hear yourself speak. Not surprisingly, the pub is popular with Skipton's inhabitants, as well as passing narrowboaters.

PEAK FOREST CANAL
AND MACCLESFIELD CANAL

Whaley Bridge to Dukinfield Junction: 14.5 miles/16 locks/2 tunnels
Macclesfield Canal, Hall Green to Marple: 27.75 miles/13 locks

The upper section of the Peak Forest Canal, from Whaley Bridge to Marple, wins all the plaudits for scenery, as it clings precariously to the side of the Goyt Valley, offering superb views of the Peak District hills to the east. A diversion to Bugsworth Basins, restored a few years back, is strongly recommended, whilst Whaley Bridge is a thoroughly enjoyable town in which to linger.

The lower section of the canal forms part of the Cheshire Ring circuit. Marple Locks, restored in the 1970s, are well kept and enjoyable to work through whilst Marple Aqueduct is another impressive feat of engineering, carrying the canal 100 feet over the wooded valley of the River Goyt. Thereafter, although you're on a level pound, it's all downhill, at least in aesthetic terms, as the canal leaves the Peak District hills behind to becomes engulfed in the Manchester conurbation.

Macclesfield Canal

Part of the popular Cheshire Ring, the Macclesfield Canal is a delight in its own right, slicing its way decisively through rugged East Cheshire countryside. Scenically it's up there with the best of them, not least in the vicinity of Bosley Locks, one of the finest flights on the system.

From the southern end of the canal there are fine views of Mow Cop to the south-west, whilst Little Moreton Hall – one of the nation's great half-timbered buildings – lies within a short walk of Bridge 85. Congleton, Macclesfield and Bollington are fine Cheshire towns all worthy of exploration.

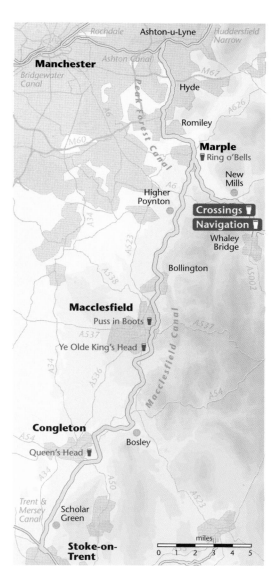

At Marple the 'Macc' joins the Peak Forest Canal at an immensely photogenic junction.

THE CROSSINGS

Furness Vale, High Peak, Derbyshire

The Peak Forest Canal is superb. It runs from Whaley Bridge through Furness Vale, New Mills and Disley to Marple. The Macclesfield Canal goes off to the left while the Peak Forest continues down the Marple flight, crosses the imposing aqueduct over the River Goyt and onwards to Ashton via Romiley, Woodley, Hyde and Dukinfield.

The section from Marple to Whaley Bridge is magical. It's built on an embankment with magnificent views down into the Goyt Valley. As you approach

Furness Vale, the canal, river, the A6 and two railways are running abreast of each other. You will see Eccles Pike directly ahead rising up 1200 feet. But try and keep your eye on the navigation as well and watch out for Bridge 31.

The first thing you will notice is Furness Vale Station with its level crossing alongside. Tucked neatly behind it are the Crossings. Originally called the Station Hotel, it was built in the mid-nineteenth century to provide sustenance for travellers on the Manchester

PUB FACTS

Location	Station Road, Furness Vale, High Peak, Derbyshire SK23 7Q9
Tel	01663 743642
Email	peter@thecrossingspub.com
Tenants	Peter Rothwell
Opening hours	Mon–Thu 12pm–3pm, 4.30pm–2am, Fri–Sun 12pm–2am
Food served	Mon–Sat lunchtime: soups and sandwiches, evenings: different menu each night, Sun Breakfast Club 10am–12pm, roast meat baps 2pm–5pm, free roast potatoes at around 5pm
Real ales	Robinson's Hatters Original and Robinson's Unicorn, plus seasonal ales
Moorings	On towpath near Furness Bridge (No 31)

to Buxton line. There used to be a station master called Jack Bramall who, when the train pulled in, instead of shouting out "Furness Vale", enticed passengers with the cry of "Finest Ale". While the engine was watering up, there would be a flurry of rail travellers watering themselves up at the pub.

People still come from Buxton and Hazel Grove to visit. And they, like boat travellers, are greeted by Peter and his locals. They'll ask you a few questions ("Are you visiting?" "Are you working here?" "Are you moving in?") and, within a few minutes, you'll either be sitting on a bar stool, chatting and sampling the excellent beers, or you'll be ensconced in one of the comfy sofas, watching the antics of the fish in the aquarium. You'll hear stories about when the pool room was a shop and when the landlady in the Second World War used to go up into the attic of the pub during the blackout, look down the valley through a slit in a little window and watch Manchester being bombed.

They are a bit sports mad in this pub. They mainly support England, whether it be football, cricket, rugby or curling (I think they've got a bit confused on the last one), but you will hear hearty cheering for Manchester United, Manchester City ("We have no trouble here") and Sale Sharks as well.

Food's important as well: Monday is Chilli Night, Tuesday Pie Night, Wednesday Bangers & Mash, Thursday Curry and Friday Casserole. All in all, the Crossings is a pub without frills, but with an exceptionally welcoming landlord and cheery locals of all ages.

NAVIGATION INN

Buxworth, High Peak, Derbyshire

Bugsworth may well have changed its name to Buxworth but below the village, the name Bugsworth is still happily used. Bugsworth Basin was built in the late 1790s to connect with the tramway from Dove Holes. The main material to be transported was limestone. This was brought down inclined planes by horse drawn wagons, and then transferred to narrowboats or burnt into lime in the kilns situated in the basin and then boated out. In 1831, the Cromford

& High Peak Railway was opened and then the wagons were hauled from the Cromford Canal to the Peak Forest by stationary or tenacious steam engines.

What a sight it must have been in Bugsworth Basin in the heyday of the canal – it was called 'the biggest port in the Kingdom' and boats were carrying out over 100,000 tons a year of limestone, lime, gritstone flags, stone setts and building stone. The kilns, the mines and the quarries would have scarred the countryside.

Inevitably, the basin fell into decline in the 1920s and nature again took the upper hand. Now, it is a delightfully peaceful haven and, thanks mainly to the many years of work by the Inland Waterways Protection Society, is again restored and open for boat traffic.

It is a fascinating place to visit, made all the better by the Navigation Inn, which is situated alongside the upper basin. It was built at the same time as the canal as a

Pub facts

Location	Brookside, Buxworth, High Peak, Derbyshire SK23 7NE
Tel	01663 732072
Email	lisa@navigationinn.co.uk
Website	www.navigationinn.co.uk
Lessee	Lisa Garner
Opening hours	Mon–Sat 11am–12am, Sun 12pm–12am
Food served	Mon–Fri 12pm–3pm, 6pm–9pm, Sat/Sun 12pm–9pm (Prices from £3.50–£12.95)
Real ales	Timothy Taylor's Landlord, Marstons' Burton Bitter, Marstons' Pedigree, Theakston's Best Bitter, plus at least one guest beer
Moorings	In the canal basin outside the pub
Rooms	5 rooms from £35 B&B

farm pub, shop and stables. The stables fell into disuse but the shop lasted until the late 1960s. It was at this time that Pat Phoenix, of Coronation Street's Elsie Tanner fame, owned the pub and, even today, coach parties arrive from Canada and New Zealand, who are members of the Coronation Street fan club. The only hint of that period is a piano on which Pat used to entertain the customers.

The Navigation caters equally for the local community and visiting boaters, walkers, cyclists and motorists. It has lots of interesting spaces: an entrance lobby with leaflets and local information and a board advertising local farm eggs for sale at a 'cheep price'; and a bar devoted to canal memorabilia with fascinating photos, the side of the ice breaker, *Shackleton*, on the wall and seats with names of canal companies. There's another bar with local history and the story of Buxworth's twinning with Clayton in California. In 1812, a family of ten set off for America from Buxworth, journeyed over the Rockies, settled in California and founded a mining industry. People from the town named after them regularly visit Buxworth and the Navigation.

The real ale's pretty good. Try one of their guest beers, like Lord Marples from Bakewell or Navigation Ale from Cornwall. And the food is all freshly prepared and features a fish board and specials.

There is a lovely paved area outside the pub and a children's playground. If you are there at the end of June, you may catch the well dressing ceremony in the basin. Locals will have been working for weeks on the decorations, which all have to be made of natural materials, like flowers, petals or wool. Derbyshire is the only county where these ceremonies take place. Originally pagan, they are now blessed by the local vicar.

The Navigation Inn claims to be probably the best pub in the world – real ales, real fires, real food, real atmosphere. It's certainly well in contention. Try it out.

OTHER PUBS WORTH TRYING

Peak Forest Canal and Macclesfield Canal

RING O' BELLS

Marple, Cheshire
130 Church Lane, Marple,
Cheshire SK6 7AY
Tel: 0161 427 2300
www.ring-o-bells.com

(Macclesfield Canal)

Marple Junction is a classic canal view and the friendly Ring o' Bells is just a stone's throw away. The beer comes from Robinson's, the (still family-owned) Stockport brewery that's an institution in these parts. The pub boasts a waterway-themed snug and a large beer terrace overlooking the canal. Take a walk down the locks and across the aqueduct to work up an appetite, then come back and spoil yourself with the expansive menu.

PUSS IN BOOTS

Macclesfield, Cheshire
198 Buxton Road, Macclesfield,
Cheshire SK10 1NF
Tel: 01625 423261

(Macclesfield Canal)

By the canal at Bridge 37, this traditional stone-built coaching inn is a proper local with easy moorings and well-kept beer. Sit on the towpath and watch the world go by.

QUEEN'S HEAD

Congleton, Cheshire
Park Lane, Congleton,
Cheshire CW12 3DE
Tel: 01260 272546
www.queensheadhotel.org.uk

(Macclesfield Canal)

Real ale aficionados will think they've died and gone to heaven, with up to seven ales on tap, a brace of CAMRA awards, and traditional pub games such as shove ha'penny. There's B&B if you're not arriving by boat – ideal for a long weekend's walking in the local hills. Sit in the large canalside beer garden and enjoy the excellent home-made food: cottage pie is the speciality.

YE OLDE KING'S HEAD   *(Macclesfield Canal)*

Gurnett, Macclesfield, Cheshire
Byrons Lane, Gurnett, Macclesfield,
Cheshire SK11 0HD
Tel: 01625 423890

The Macclesfield Canal is not one to let such trifling matters as geography stand in its course, and the aqueduct by this friendly village pub is one of the many means by which it keeps a level as it strides across the countryside. The traditional pub food is of good quality and, for those arriving by boat, mooring is easy.

TRENT & MERSEY CANAL

Derwentmouth Lock to Preston Brook
93 miles/76 locks/4 tunnels

Mostly rural, always characterful, occasionally beautiful, the Trent & Mersey is a distinguished canal well worthy of exploration. From the Trent near Shardlow it runs to the Bridgewater Canal at Preston Brook, and features broad locks as far as Burton-on-Trent, a compact town famous for its breweries.

Fradley Junction, where the Coventry Canal heads off to the south, is as pretty as a picture, with its canalside cottages and popular pub. Remote woodlands accompany the canal through to Rugeley, a workaday town, useful for shopping.

The finest section of the T&M comes as it skirts Cannock Chase. From Great Haywood you can visit Shugborough Hall and Park. Access from the canal is by way of the 14-arched Essex Bridge over the Trent.

Through Stoke-on-Trent the canal threads its way forlornly through a strange kind of no man's land: not rural, but no longer industrial.

Harecastle Tunnel – all 2,897 yards of it – leads on to 'Heartbreak Hill' where the canal drops down through 32 locks, many of them duplicated, in the space of just 12 miles. Beyond Middlewich the T&M continues through surprisingly pleasant open country and onto the remarkable Anderton Boat Lift – one of the 'Seven Wonders of the Waterways' – where you can if you choose descend to the River Weaver.

The Trent & Mersey ends its 93-mile journey from Derwentmouth at Preston Brook, where it joins the Bridgewater Canal.

For pubs on the Caldon Canal, see page 7.

STANLEY ARMS

Anderton, near Northwich, Cheshire

PUB FACTS

Location	Old Road, Anderton, near Northwich, Cheshire CW9 6AG
Tel	01606 75059
Email	mccafferty375@btinternet.com
Landlords	Mick & Angela McCafferty
Opening hours	Mon–Sat 12pm–11pm, Sun 12pm–10.30pm
Food served	Mon–Sat 12pm–9pm, Sun 12pm–7pm (anything from a cheese sandwich to a mixed grill)
Real ales	John Smiths, Greene King IPA, Old Speckled Hen
Moorings	Some outside pub plus opposite on towpath side

The Stanley Arms looks down on the Anderton Boat Lift. It was the very first boat lift in the world, opening in 1875, to allow boats to travel between the Trent & Mersey Canal and the River Weaver.

However, the pub was not built either for the canal or for the boat lift. It opened in 1753 as the Stanley Arms Hotel. Sir John Stanley and his family owned vast tracts of land in the area. The family motto was Sans Changer ("Without Changing"), still to be seen on the coat of arms which is part of the pub sign. The hotel was an inn and no spirits were allowed to be served. It was there to service farm workers with a frothing glass of ale and, perhaps, a hunk of bread and cheese (Cheshire, of course).

This quiet rural pub began a new life in 1777, when the Trent & Mersey Canal opened and passed by immediately below it. It then became the haunt of boatpeople and, in 1793, grew even busier when cargoes began to be transhipped from narrowboats to the barges fifty feet below on the River Weaver. By the turn of the eighteenth century, two salt chutes and an inclined plane were in operation mainly offloading salt from the

canal to the barges tied up on the Weaver. That was when the Stanley Arms got nicknamed the Tip.

It soon became apparent that the time and energy put into transhipment was not cost effective and, with true Victorian aplomb, the trustees of the Weaver navigation gave the go ahead to the building of a unique vertical hydraulic boat lift, in which the boats themselves would descend with their cargoes to the river below and vice versa. It was an engineering masterpiece and proved highly successful, changing to electric operation in 1908.

The Anderton Boat Lift remained operational until 1983, when the ravages of time and the corrosion of the structure, due to the brine in the water and chemical pollution, led to its closure. In 2002, the boat lift re-opened for what is now exclusively pleasure traffic.

The pub today is much larger than the one room pub of the 18th century. There is a conservatory and benches, and children's games on what used to be the putting green and, before that, a crown bowling green. Boats tie up on the canal below and provide the pub with much of its trade, although its local trade boasts a darts, dominoes and football team.

There are canal paintings everywhere inside the pub to remind us of the past and etched glass windows at the front of the pub, one of which says Smoking Room. That is also history.

THE COMMERCIAL HOTEL

Wheelock, Cheshire

PUB FACTS

Location	2 Game Street, Wheelock, Cheshire, CW11 3RR (off Crewe Road, on the square by the canal bridge)
Tel	01270 760122
Landlady	Judy Atkinson
Opening hours	Mon–Thu 3.30pm–11pm, Fri–Sun 12pm–11pm
Food served	Filled baps
Real ales	Weetwood Best Bitter, Thwaites Bitter and guest beers
Moorings	On towpath side above the water point

The wharf at Wheelock on the Trent & Mersey Canal is a very convenient stopping off point if you are boating. You have either descended or are about to tackle the Cheshire Locks or 'Heartbreak Hill', 26 locks between Wheelock and Hardings Wood, just outside Kidsgrove. So, you'll either need to refresh yourselves or take stock before the climb – water up, empty the loo and discard your rubbish, do a bit of shopping and grab a pint or two. The Cheshire Cheese on the wharf looks inviting and is certainly worth a visit, but cross the road and you will discover a listed Georgian gem.

Not that it has always been a pub. It was built as a house for one of the managers at the ironworks somewhere between 1750 and 1770. But, before 1800, it was converted into a public house. There was an article in a newspaper of 1816 describing the pub as having stabling for 50 horses and a granary, and that one of the principal traffics on the canal was Cheshire cheeses for London. Coaches stopped at the pub, as it was part of the route between Manchester and Shrewsbury and a new turnpike road was being built between Nantwich and Wheelock.

Until relatively recently, the Commercial had been run by the same family for over 70 years. Lennie Davies became the landlord in 1922. A few years later, his daughter, Judy, was born and she lived there until her retirement.

The 1930s sound as if they would have been good times to be a local at the Commercial. The last wedding reception was held in the functions room in 1930 but Lennie then started musical concerts. He bought the now famous basket chairs, built a little stage and, every month, it was packed with folk listening to gramophone records played by one of the first DJs. There was even a printed programme listing the items that were to be enjoyed.

There is a timeless feel to this pub, and Judy kept it pretty much as it was when she took over from her dad. It has an open bar area and two small, cosy rooms off it, as well as the functions/games room. Even the current landlady, the 'new' Judy, has made very few changes – a lick of paint here and there, a public phone and a few baps on sale. Oh, and the garden at the back has been opened to customers.

But the pre-war handpumps are still there and the basket chairs are used in the bar and the snug. Though they're not in the little lounge anymore, they are always brought out for functions. I think Lennie would be pleased.

OTHER PUBS WORTH TRYING
Trent & Mersey Canal

BLUE BELL
Kidsgrove, Stoke-on-Trent
25 Hardingswood, Kidsgrove,
Stoke-on-Trent, ST7 1EG
Tel: 01782 774052
www.bluebellkidsgrove.co.uk

A quiet but sociable pub (there are deliberately no jukeboxes, TVs or games machines) serves a range of cask beers and bottled continental lagers. Do take a wander outside, too, to 'gongoozle' at the intricate Hardings Wood Junction.

SWAN INN

Stone, Staffordshire
18 Stafford Street, Stone,
Staffordshire ST15 8QW
Tel: 01785 815570

A lively and traditional pub, popular with locals and boaters alike, in a Grade II listed building that was formerly a warehouse during the construction of the canal. An extensive range of guest beers is available. There is regular live music and a beer festival during the second week of July.

SPODE COTTAGE

Armitage, Staffordshire
Lower Lodge, Rugeley Road, Armitage,
Rugeley, Staffordshire WS15 4AT
Tel: 01543 490353

Refurbished in 2006, this Elizabethan pub on the outskirts of Rugeley has a large canalside beer garden with children's play area. Food is themed: steak night, fish & chip night, lunchtime and weekend carveries etc. Plenty of draught beers too.

SWAN

Fradley, Staffordsire
Fradley Junction, Alrewas,
Burton-on-Trent, Staffs DE13 7DN
Tel: 01283 790330

Something of a tourist trap on fine weekends, visitors come to watch the activity at one of the canal network's busiest junctions and to enjoy the pub's home-cooked food (lunchtimes and evenings) and a good range of beers.

MALT SHOVEL

Shardlow, Derbyshire
The Wharf, Shardlow,
Derbyshire DE72 2HG
Tel: 01332 799763

Warm and snug in winter with a roaring log fire and lots of tables for two – ideal for romantic couples! In summer watch the boating activity from the seats outside. A good range of beers, excellent food and friendly staff – one of the T&M's nicest pubs.

CLOCK WAREHOUSE

Shardlow, Derbyshire
London Road, Shardlow, Derbyshire
DE72 2GL
Tel: 01332 792844

Immensely popular in summer, the Clock Warehouse probably attracts more diners than drinkers for its hearty pub grub. The refurbished former grain warehouse offers a varied menu and pleasant surroundings; there's also a skittle alley, plus, of course, the adjacent Shardlow Heritage Centre in which to absorb a little of the area's canal history.

RIVER AVON (WARWICKSHIRE)

Tewkesbury to Stratford
42 miles/17 locks

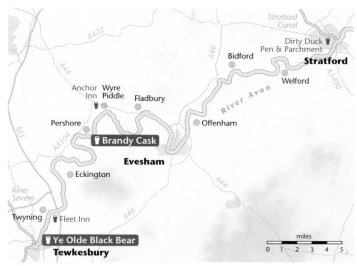

If you were entertaining overseas visitors and wished to show them a slice of England at its best, you could do worse than take them on a trip along Shakespeare's Avon. The river drifts deliciously through a seemingly timeless landscape, its progress punctuated by a series of immaculate towns and villages.

Tewkesbury – a classic English country town – sets the tone for this most memorable of river voyages. Passing Bredon Hill and 16th century Eckington Bridge, you arrive at Pershore, a Georgian town of immense charm, best known perhaps for its tasty red plums. Evesham, some 11 miles upstream, marks the boundary between the Lower and Upper navigable sections of the river and boasts a fine waterfront and lots of nice restaurants and tearooms.

Henceforth the river adopts a somewhat less manicured air, but its loveliness is omnipresent. Bidford – weekend playground of West Midlanders – offers excellent moorings and good facilities and then you're on the final approach to Stratford. To arrive in this internationally renowned town by boat represents one of the great inland waterway experiences. You can moor right opposite the Royal Shakespeare Theatre. There are super shops, plush restaurants, cosy tearooms, museums, open top bus trips, the list goes on and on. You can even go for a towpath walk along the Stratford Canal as it begins its journey towards Birmingham. Enjoy your time in Stratford!

The Avon is navigable for a further three miles or so up to Alveston. In the early 1980s plans were published advocating extension of the navigable section up to Warwick, some ten miles distant, where a link could be made with the Grand Union Canal. Wealthy riparian landowners wasted no time in blowing the whistle on these plans and a potentially exciting project was stillborn.

The Warwickshire Avon at Stratford.

THE BRANDY CASK
PUB & BREWERY

Pershore, Worcestershire

The Vale of Evesham: this immediately conjures up pictures of rolling countryside with orchards and fields full of vegetables, and English asparagus (the best), and towns and villages asking to be visited for their antiquity and charm.

Pershore is a classic example. Renowned not only for its Abbey and for its beautiful Georgian town houses but for its plum, discovered growing wild nearby in 1833. Take a stroll down Bridge Street and you'll know you're in Pershore when you stop outside the Brandy Cask - it's the only pub of that name in Britain.

If you're lucky enough to arrive by boat in Pershore, watch out for the Brandy Cask's mooring, just opposite Pershore Lock. Very new and very smart, it's at the bottom

of a beautifully kept long garden complete with a Victorian rose arch, raised and sunken gardens, conifer garden, rockery, patios and a pond containing some very large, colourful fish.

Spencer and Marianne are responsible for all this and for the pub itself. They bought it in 1990 and, after they moved in, began to discover the fascinating story of the site. The rear part of the building was built in medieval times and was probably a wool warehouse. The Georgian frontage was erected in 1779, when Henry J. Baker converted the building into a house and liquor vault. Barrels of beer, wine and spirits (including much brandy – hence the name of the pub) were trundled into the vault. The contents were bottled and delivered to the local gentry by horse and cart. The less well off had to do with turning up at a little off-sales window to fill their jug.

The Bakers continued to live in and work from the building until 1920, when it was bought by Hunt Edmunds Brewery of Banbury, converted into a pub and named the Brandy Cask.

By the time of the Second World War, the Berrys were the tenants. On 29th May 1943, Mrs Berry was standing at the front door of her pub watching a fly past of aeroplanes, celebrating the £100,000 collected by the people of Pershore in a Wings for Victory Appeal. A Wellington bomber lost an engine. The engine hit the tail-plane, the aircraft plummeted into the front of the pub, landed halfway down the garden and burst into flames. Poor Mrs Berry was hit by slates from the roof but survived relatively intact, but the two Canadian pilots and three British ground crew on for the ride were killed. A plaque outside the pub commemorates the event.

In 1995, Spencer thought it would be a good idea to have a go at "this brewing lark" and established a brewery in one of the outhouses. The beers quickly enhanced the pub's reputation with such delights as his best seller, Brandy Snapper at 4%, a pale, hoppy old-fashioned bitter, or the seasonal Ale Mary, a strong bitter, tasting of malt, fruit and hops.

Every day, you can eat freshly-cooked food, with a traditional roast on a Sunday. Soon you'll be able to stay in one of their ten new bedrooms.

Pub facts

Location	25 Bridge Street, Pershore, Worcestershire WR10 1AJ
Tel/Fax	01386 552602
Website	www.brandycask.pershoretown.com
Proprietors/ Landlords	Spencer & Marianne Cooper
Opening hours	Mon–Wed 11.30am–2.30pm, 7pm–11pm, Thu–Sat 11.30am–3pm, 7pm–11.30pm, Sun 12pm–3pm, 7pm–11pm
Food served	daily 12pm–2pm, 7pm–9pm
Real ales	Whistling Joe, Brandy Snapper, John Baker's Original, plus seasonal beers, eg. Ale Mary
Moorings	At the bottom of the pub garden opposite Pershore Lock or further along adjoining the playing fields and leisure centre

Ye Olde Black Bear

Tewkesbury, Gloucestershire

Tewkesbury, with its beautiful Abbey and half-timbered houses, demands to be visited. So, if you're on a boat, get tied up and start with a visit to the Ye Olde Black Bear, the oldest pub in Gloucestershire and the fifth oldest in the country.

Beer has been served here since 1308 and the name originates from the bear and ragged staff motif of the arms of the Beauchamp family, the Earls of Warwick who held the Manor of Tewkesbury. It's Grade II* listed, with a special listing for the leather ceiling in the bar, embossed with Tudor roses and green and gilt fishes. Said to have been made by Italian monks to pay for their lodging while working at the Abbey, it dates from the 16th century and is one of only ten in the country. Sit under that ceiling in what was the original bar, look out of the window and imagine what you might have seen in years past. – maybe people being hanged from the tree opposite or stuck in the stocks.

The pub has little bars everywhere and cosy corners. The low-beamed snug with its collection of old photos, paintings and prints used to be the area where the coaches pulled in to change horses on their journey to Bristol or Manchester. The restaurant was the stables, where, during the Battle of Tewkesbury in 1471, the penultimate battle in the Wars of the Roses, the routed Lancastrians found refuge for the dying and the injured.

So, of course, this pub has ghosts – with a vengeance. Remember all those dying routed Lancastrians? Well, every 5th May, the night after that battle, the screams of those poor men can be heard in the restaurant, so they say. Okay, what about the cavalier who walks around one of the bedrooms, searching for the space in the attic where they used to hide from the Roundheads. And the little boy with light brown hair cut in a page-boy bob, who wanders around the building looking for the tunnel which led from the pub to the Abbey. In 1945, when they were demolishing the dairy to make the beer garden, a cellar was

PUB FACTS

Location	68 High Street, Tewkesbury, Gloucestershire GL20 5BJ
Tel	01684 292202
Managers	Paul & April Wallis
Email	pwallisfamily@aol.com
Opening	Mon–Sat 11am–11pm, Sun 12pm–10.30pm
Food	12pm–9pm
Real ales	Adnams Bitter, Adnams Broadside, Wells Bombardier plus two changing guest beers, eg Lancaster Bomber and Wicked Witch
Moorings	At the bottom of the pub garden or on the opposite bank

discovered with a trapdoor in it, which led to another cellar and to what appeared to be the entrance of a tunnel, now blocked with earth after a few yards. The way to the Abbey?

With a shiver, I discovered that an old lady in Victorian clothes comes and sits in the very seat I was sitting in, every evening. Many people have seen her or felt her presence. There's also a horseshoe on the wall of the old stable which every five years ends up on the other side of the river. A ghost with a tantrum or a jokey regular? And what about the light bulbs? Every week, all over the building, 20 or 30 of them have to be changed. A ghost who prefers the dark – or just very bad, old wiring?

Chefs, Gerard and Johnny, like their food and serve up award-winning sausages; chicken, cheese and bacon melts; Chicken Kiev; and profiterolles.

If you can, visit the pub in the evening: join the regulars in a quiz by a log fire in the winter or in the summer sit in the riverside garden watching morris dancing. Even if you come by car, you no longer have the problem of fording the river. John, who was to become King, built the first bridge by the tavern in 1200.

OTHER PUBS WORTH TRYING

River Avon

PEN & PARCHMENT

Stratford, Warwickshire
Bridgefoot, Stratford-upon-Avon,
Warwickshire CV37 6YY
Tel: 01789 297697
www.thepenandparchment.com

Beautifully situated twixt canal and river, predictably popular with tourists. Brace yourself for crowds on a summer's day, or catch it off-season for a quiet pint. Flooding in 2007 – the curse of any riverside pub – has meant a complete refurbishment. Plenty of outdoor seating and respectable, though far from imaginative, food and beer.

DIRTY DUCK

Stratford, Warwickshire
Waterside, Stratford-upon-Avon,
Warwickshire CV37 6BA
Tel: 01789 297312
www.dirty-duck.co.uk

The full Stratford experience. Housed in a 15th century building and situated next door to the Royal Shakespeare Company (nothing on Mikron, of course), this pub is well-known in theatre circles and you may find yourself rubbing shoulders with the great and the good. There's a riverside terrace and, believe it or not, a "walled Pimms garden".

ANCHOR INN

Wyre Piddle, Worcestershire
Wyre Piddle, Pershore,
Worcestershire WR10 2JB
Tel: 01386 556059
www.anchorwyrepiddle.co.uk

Wyre Piddle might have a slightly daft name, but it's a lovely village, full of half-timbered houses: and the Anchor fits right in. Its attractive stepped beer garden runs down to the banks of the Avon, giving excellent views of passing cruisers. The traditional ales include those from the Wyre Piddle Brewery – Piddle in the Snow, Piddle in the Wind, etc. A great pub for your Sunday lunch.

FLEET INN

Twyning Fleet, Gloucestershire
Twyning, Tewkesbury,
Gloucestershire GL20 6FL
Tel: 01684 274310
www.fleet-inn.co.uk

For years the site of a ferry across the river. Today the pub, down a little village lane, feels like the 'end of nowhere', yet is easily accessible from M50 junction 1 and worth the detour. Decent food – try the steak baguettes – is available in a tangle of rooms and bars; the pictures in the boaters' bar are worth a look. The riverside seating is lovely on a summer's day, and do take a look at the Siberian chipmunks!

BIRMINGHAM CANAL NAVIGATIONS

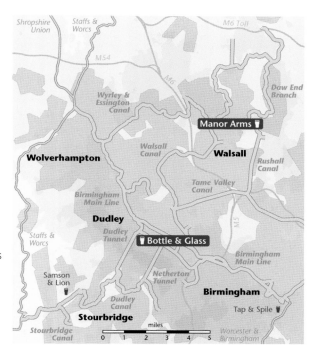

Once at the heart of the industrial revolution, the BCN provided Birmingham and the Black Country with its first heavy freight transport system, with over 160 miles and 200 locks. More than 100 miles are left to cruise today providing the chance to experience some magnificent industrial archaeology and amazing 21st century developments.

The principal area for boats is the main line from central Birmingham towards Wolverhampton. In the Gas Street/ Farmers Bridge area the old factories and businesses have been replaced by the International Convention Centre, the National Indoor Arena and the Sealife Centre; thus the canals have been re-introduced to locals. The rebuilt Bull Ring area and Mailbox development extend futuristic structures round Salvage Turn on the Worcester & Birmingham Canal. Ample moorings allow boaters to visit the numerous restaurants, bars and department stores.

From Farmers Bridge Junction the canal strides away in a substantially straight line. Branches that lead off were the original looping course, straightened by Thomas Telford in the early 1800s, reducing the distance between Wolverhampton and Birmingham from 22½ to 15 miles.

At Smethwick the old line bears to the right and up a flight of locks, the new line carries on ahead. The old crosses its successor on a rare canal-over-canal aqueduct only to repeat the feat over the Netherton Tunnel branch en route to Tipton.

Pudding Green Junction gives access to the Wednesbury Old and Walsall canals. A left turn at Dudley Port Junction leads to Netherton Tunnel, a huge, once gas-lit cavern leading to Halesowen, the Dudley canals and Stourbridge. After three locks, a left turn at Factory Junction leads to the Black Country Museum at Dudley. This is the Old Main Line, last seen ascending Smethwick Locks, the winding original route between the two junctions thought by many to be more interesting than the new direct main line.

Northwards from Coseley a short tunnel is followed by Deepfields Junction; turn right for the Wednesbury Oak 'loop'. On the edge of Wolverhampton is Horseley Fields Junction, with the Wyrley & Essington to the right. Ahead, central Wolverhampton moorings are followed by 21 locks down to the Staffordshire & Worcestershire Canal.

The rest of the BCN holds a compelling fascination for some canal enthusiasts but are an acquired taste. The scenery varies from heavily built up to the wide spaces on the edge of Cannock Chase.

BOTTLE & GLASS INN

Dudley, West Midlands

PUB FACTS

Location	Black Country Living Museum, Tipton Road, Dudley, West Midlands DY1 4SQ
Tel	0121 557 9643 for information 0121 557 8054 group bookings Fax 0121 557 4242
Email	info@bclm.co.uk
Website	www.bclm.co.uk
Opening hours	Museum 10am–5pm, Pub 11am–4pm (3pm winter
Food	Cheese & onion cobs only
Real ales	Banks's Bitter, Mansfield Dark Mild and guest ales including those from the Olde Swan Brewery, Netherton
Moorings	Outside the back of the pub

In its heyday, the Bottle & Glass Inn was frequented by miners, glass cutters and, particularly, boatmen who would sometimes be tempted to linger there from opening time at nine in the morning until late in the evening. Their horses grazed happily on the garden at the back of the pub, while their masters often ended up in a contentious brawl. 'Nice women' stayed away.

Not a pub really to recommend to you good-living readers, you would think. But no. You must visit. Nothing much has changed. Well, that's not strictly true. The pub has moved for a start.

Originally called the Bush, it was built backing on to the Sixteen Locks on the Stourbridge Canal in Brockmoor, shortly after their completion in 1779. By the 1840s, it had become the Bottle & Glass Inn. It closed in 1979. It was then presented to the Black Country Museum, moved to Dudley and reassembled, brick by brick.

So its site has changed and so has the clientele. You don't meet many miners or glasscutters, although an encounter with a boatman, albeit well scrubbed up, is likely as the pub is now situated alongside the Dudley No1 Canal on the approach to Dudley Tunnel. But the pub still looks and feels as it did in the early 1900s.

There's the bar with its original bench seating, handpumps and spittoons and, yes, there's sawdust on the floor. In 1910, this was the working man's territory and woe betide any manager who ventured in there. Glasses would be banged down, arms folded and there would be what can only be described as a 'loud silence'.

Women were discouraged, except those who sat on the bench by the fire and charged for their company. Soliciting was illegal; so, they chalked their price on the soles of their boots, which they would ensure were visible. When they'd secured a customer, they would erase the evidence in the sawdust on their way out.

The landlady reigned supreme. The pub was the hub of the community, and she would mete out justice to men who drank their wages away. No man answered back when she said, "Off 'ome now. Sort yer kids out."

You won't be able to sample the small beer (or baby beer as it was known locally). It was only about 2%, which was just as well as the foundry workers used to drink as much as 24 pints a day. But Debbie, the current landlady, will pull you a fine pint of local real ale. There is, of course, no lager. When asked for it, Debbie will offer the customer an empty glass and suggest they fill it from the canal: "It's just as good for you."

Next door is the snug where the foremen would drink, and at the back is the parlour with its piano, aspidistras and paintings of fighting cocks. There the managers would be able to ring for service. I warn you. The bell is no longer operational.

Tie up your boat, pay your money and have a wonderful day out. Have a ride on a tram, a trip into Dudley Tunnel, go down a coal mine but don't, on any account, fail to visit - several times if possible - the Bottle & Glass Inn.

MANOR ARMS

Rushall, Walsall, West Midlands

PUB FACTS

Location	Park Road, Rushall, Walsall, West Midlands WS4 ILG
Tel	01922 642333
Lessees	Maggie Bradshaw & Martin Knight
Manager	Derek Hart
Opening hours	Mon–Sat 12pm–12am, Sun 12pm–11pm
Food served	Mon–Sat 12pm–2.30pm, 5pm–7.30pm, Sun 12.30pm–5pm
Real ales	Banks's Original, Banks's Bitter, Jenning's Cocker Hoop
Moorings	Outside the pub

The regulars at the Manor Arms were in an exultant mood. It was 1.30pm on 8th May 1945 and it was VE Day. After a few pints, it was agreed with the jovial landlord, Bill Harley, that the wives would join them in the evening for a celebratory fish and chip supper and a sing-song. Out of the window, they could see lightning and heavy rain. Suddenly, there was a mighty flash and what sounded like a bomb going off. It was, in fact, a thunderbolt hitting the pub. The fireplace in the lounge collapsed and bricks, soot and debris engulfed the room and its astonished occupants. Amazingly, no one was hurt; so, they immediately set about clearing the place up. The fish and chip supper was off but they all managed to down a few more pints and have a song or two. A cartoon of the day had one of the locals saying, with bricks flying around him: "Bloody hell, this beer's got a kick today".

Nothing much has changed since then. I don't mean the pub is continually being hit by thunderbolts, but it does remain a very friendly, very old-fashioned pub. It has three small rooms and a passageway, where customers stand and drink and they are served through a hatch. There is no bar counter but, in one of the rooms, the beer is served from a bank of hand pumps mounted on the wall. This is where the Geriatric Club meets almost every day, a group of oldies – all reputedly millionaires! – to discuss matters of the world. There is no music anywhere in the pub, by the way; so, you can join in, as I did, with the locals and hear them tell stories about the War, when Glenn Miller, the bandleader, was one of the regulars.

The original building dates back to 1104 and has had a licence since 1248. At one point, it was a mill house and, in the fourteenth century, it was lived in by monks. Since the eighteenth century, it has been a pub, originally with stables to service the canal.

The large garden is alongside the Daw End Branch that runs from

Catshill to Longwood on the northern BCN (Birmingham Canal Navigations). Surprisingly, it is very rural and links the Wyrley & Essington to the Rushall Canal. It's a contour canal built to carry limestone from the nearby workings to feed the Black Country's hungry furnaces.

Tie up at the pub (you'll find it near Daw End Bridge), or arrive by car, bike or foot and sample the atmosphere, the beers and the scrumptious home-made food, like steak and ale pie, curries and chillies. Then walk off the excess with a stroll round the nearby Park Lime Pits, an old mining area which is now a nature reserve with pools and wet grassland, and say to yourself, "So this is the Black Country. Wow!"

OTHER PUBS WORTH TRYING

Birmingham Canal Navigation

TAP & SPILE

Birmingham

Gas Street Birmingham B1 2JT

Tel: 0121 632 5602

www.tapandspilebirmingham.co.uk

Looking out directly onto Gas Street Basin, the heart of Birmingham's canals, the Tap & Spile's real beer and worn furniture is a welcome respite from the commerce and glitz of the Second City. Also try the next-door Canalside Café which has an alcohol licence and knows how to use it.

SAMSON & LION

Wordsley, West Midlands

140 Brierley Hill Road, Wordsley, Stourbridge, West Midlands DY8 5SP

Tel: 01384 77796

www.samsonandlion.co.uk

(Stourbridge Canal)

A traditional Black Country alehouse, the 'Sammie' has five real ales and a wide range of entertainment, including a skittle alley. The restaurant, Delilah's, is rather more ambitious than you might think for such a pub and regularly stages themed evenings; and this being the Midlands, Sunday is of course carvery day.

COVENTRY CANAL,
ASHBY CANAL AND BIRMINGHAM & FAZELEY CANAL

Coventry to Fradley Junction: 38 miles/13 locks
Marston Junction to Snarestone: 22 miles/0 locks/1 tunnnel
Fazeley Junction to Farmers Bridge Junction: 15 miles/38 locks/1 tunnel

Few people relish the prospect of being sent to Coventry, even by canal boat. However, Coventry's terminal basin – much 'tarted up' in the 1990s – is a pleasant enough spot and the city has much to inspire, not least the ruins of the medieval cathedral which stand alongside its 1962 successor.

The Coventry Canal is rather like the curate's egg: good in parts. The first few miles are industrial and a little dull, but Hawkesbury Junction (with the Oxford Canal) and Marston Junction (with the Ashby Canal) come along in swift succession to lift the spirits.

The most picturesque section of the Coventry Canal lies between Fazeley and Huddlesford junctions, especially its passage through delightful Hopwas Woods. Wide ranging views accompany the canal through the lower Tame valley, whilst the Dutch style village of Fisherwick (where the houses face on to the waterway) adds further interest; as does Whittington with its good range of amenities.

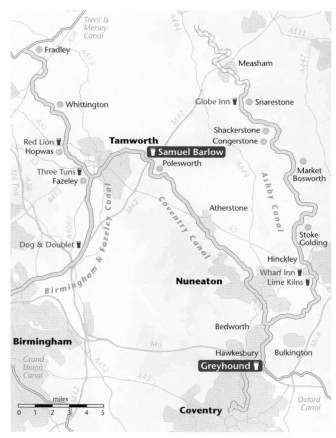

Ashby Canal

The lockless Ashby Canal traverses a gently undulating rural landscape from its junction with the Coventry Canal up to the present day terminus at Snarestone. There's much of interest to enjoy, including the Bosworth Battlefield Centre at Shenton and delightful Market Bosworth, a mile up the hill from the canal wharf.

Birmingham & Fazeley Canal

An important link between the Coventry Canal and the Birmingham Canal Navigations, this canal passes through some surprisingly attractive countryside on its 15-mile route through the West Midlands.

THE GREYHOUND

Hawkesbury Junction, Longford, Coventry, West Midlands

PUB FACTS

Location	Sutton Stop, Hawkesbury Junction, Longford, Coventry, West Midlands CV6 6DF
Tel	024 7636 3046
Licensee	Leigh Watts
Opening hours	Mon–Sat 11am–11pm, Sun 12pm–10.30pm
Food served	Mon–Sat 12pm–3pm, 6pm–9pm (Starters from £3.85–£4.25, mains from £7.50–£13.45), Sun 12pm–3pm (Sunday lunch only)
Real ales	Marston's Pedigree, Highgate Mild plus guest beers, eg York Brewery's Wild Wheat
Moorings	Outside pub

Sutton Stop at Hawkesbury Junction never fails to be a fascinating place. It is where the Coventry and North Oxford Canals meet and is dominated by a very fine cast iron bridge, which, with its 50 foot span, provides an ideal platform for gongoozlers. These are the people of all ages who gather at places on the canals where they're likely to get a bit of action – a staircase of locks like Foxton, a low bridge like Potter Heigham or a tricky junction. Here at Sutton Stop, hours of pleasure can be had watching boats attempting the ninety degree turn and marking them out of ten for their skill…or not.

The Greyhound was built in 1825 and the earliest known owner was Thomas Worthy, a farmer. He became a victualler and supplied the needs of the boatmen and their horses. Until recent

the pub, where there is also a large garden.

If it's food you're after, look no further. It's all fresh, home-cooked and delicious. The pub is famous for its pies and for its thick, hearty winter soups, available all day on the counter in the Donkey Box.

The pub attracts a colourful mix of people: canal folk, walkers and cyclists and professionals from the newly-built estates opposite. You may feel at home on the Gits Table where the Greyhound Inn Topers Society resides. Swap a tale or two with a factory owner, a lorry driver, a schoolteacher and an undertaker. There are no fruit machines, no pool tables, no loud music and no swearing. It's that sort of pub.

times, it was very much a pub for people off boats and, although its fame has spread far and wide, it still retains many of the features of the old pub – the snug, known as the Donkey Box and the tap room or the Elbow Room. There's a log fire, high backed settles and copious canal mementoes and photographs.

Leigh Watts, the licensee, takes a great pride in his beers, particularly his dark mild, of which he, amazingly, sells 100 gallons a week. There are always interesting guest beers on draught. I particularly enjoyed the Wild Wheat from York Brewery. You may be lucky enough to coincide with one of their beer festivals, which are held in April and July and feature 22 cask ales and 4 or 5 ciders. This is held in the barn at the back of

If you can tear yourself away from the Greyhound for a while, have a look around outside. It is now designated as a conservation area. Probably the first building at the junction was the toll house, erected in 1777 by the Coventry Canal Company, and then slowly a cluster of buildings developed to service the needs of the canal. By 1841, in addition to the tollhouse, there were canal offices, the Greyhound, ten cottages and the Engine House.

But the heart of Sutton Stop has always been the people: the boat people celebrating the end of the Second World War at the pub with dancing and singing, the boating visitors today from all over Europe and the local Gits having a bit of a banter. It's a great spot.

SAMUEL BARLOW

Alvecote, nr Tamworth, Staffordshire

PUB FACTS

Location	Alvecote Marina, Robey's Lane, Alvecote, nr Tamworth, Staffordshire B78 1AS
Tel	01827 898175
Email	enquiries@samuelbarlow.co.uk
Website	www.samuelbarlow.co.uk
Landlord	Andrew Burge
Opening hours	Sun–Thurs 12pm–11pm, Fri/Sat 12pm–1am
Food served	Bar: Mon–Sat 12pm–4pm, 6pm–9pm (except Mon evenings), Restaurant: Tue–Sat 6pm–9pm, Sun 12pm–4pm
Real ales	Marston's Pedigree, Samuel Barlow's, plus two guest ales
Moorings	Outside pub and on towpath side opposite

The Coventry Canal was always prosperous. It was completed in 1790 from Coventry to Fradley, although the section from Whittington Brook to Fazeley Junction was technically part of the Birmingham & Fazeley Canal. Running through the Warwickshire coalfields, coal was its major cargo. Even in 1947, the last year before most of the canals were nationalised, it was paying a dividend of 6%.

But after the Second World War, more and more coal was carried by road and rail and in Warwickshire many of the pits had become exhausted and were closing. From the 1960s onwards, people began to realise the leisure potential of the winding, narrow waterways built in the eighteenth century and it no longer seemed a daft idea to take a boat holiday along a canal with disused coalfields as part of the scenery.

Some of the transhipment basins

were turned into boatyards. One such was Alvecote Basin near bridge 59 (pronounced Allcott by the boat people).

In the '90s, Malcolm Burge decided to expand and to build a marina on the site of the old pithead. After the usual tests for subsidence and poisons, the marina was dug out and became the moorings for 175 boats. Not being one to just sit back and look at a lot of boats tied up, Malcolm considered what these boat owners and other passing boaters might require. Naturally, his first thought was… a pub!

So, he designed and built an attractive building on two floors adjacent to the marina with canalside lawns and a first floor balcony from where one could sit with a pint and watch the boats go by. It opened in 2004, with his son, Andrew, as the landlord. What did they decide to call it? The Samuel Barlow, of course, after the founder of the Samuel Barlow Coal Carrying Company Ltd. Barlows often worked out of Alvecote Basin. Ironically, he may not have approved of the pub, though. He was a teetotaller all his life.

Most people stopping off here will definitely approve. The bar is on the first floor (there is lift access). You can sit on the balcony and soak up the sunshine in summer or in front of an open fire in winter. There's a big screen where they often show canal films, like *The Bargee* and *Painted Boats*. There are always guest beers available, alongside the ever reliable Marston's Pedigree, often from small local independent breweries. And they serve sandwiches and salads.

Downstairs is the very pleasant restaurant with its canal paintings and Measham teapots. You can eat there in the evenings from Tuesday to Saturday. All the food is sourced from local butchers and vegetable shops.

The tradition of commercial narrowboating is maintained at the Samuel Barlow. The Burge family have a resplendent collection of old boats tied up including the *Sunny Valley* (built in 1899 and originally named *Northolt*), *Kangaroo, Australia, Greyhound* and *Grendon*.

In recent years, the Burge fleet have carried road stone, timber, grain, fence panels, engines and domestic fuel. They are always looking for cargoes. So, if you want anything moving, go and have a pint at the Samuel Barlow and book one of their beautiful boats.

OTHER PUBS WORTH TRYING

Coventry Canal, Birmingham & Fazeley and Ashby Canal

RED LION
Hopwas, Staffordshire
Lichfield Road, Hopwas, Tamworth,
Staffordshire B78 3AF
Tel: 01827 62514

(Coventry Canal)
An excellent, but unpretentious menu makes this pub a favourite for people from miles around. The large beer garden rolls down to the canal, and the real ale is well kept. A perfect pub for a summer afternoon.

DOG & DOUBLET
Bodymoor Heath, West Midlands
Bodymoor Heath, Sutton Coldfield,
West Midlands B76 9JD
Tel: 01827 872374

(Birmingham & Fazeley Canal)
Near the foot of the straggling Curdworth Locks, this middle-of-nowhere boatmen's pub has a great location and a dark, wood-heavy traditional feel, with a handful of towpath tables. Very popular with walkers. Simple pub grub and decent beer.

GLOBE INN
Snarestone, Leicestershire
Main Street, Snarestone,
Leicestershire DE12 7DB
Tel: 01530 270272

(Ashby Canal)
Sleepy Snarestone's premier attraction. Food is served daily, from bar snacks to full meals. There's a restaurant too, a pleasant garden and accommodation. A lovely chill-out zone after a day's boating!

THREE TUNS
Fazeley, Stafforshire
32 Watling Street, Fazeley,
Tamworth, Staffordshire B78 3QN
Tel: 01827 281620
www.threetunsfazeley.com

(Birmingham & Fazeley/Coventry Canal)
Basic but inexpensive food – lunch and evening Mon–Sat, lunch only on Sunday – makes this pub popular with locals and canal boaters alike. There's a pleasant garden, with moorings for two boats. Live music and karaoke enliven the occasional Friday evening.

LIME KILNS
Hinckley, Leicestershire
Watling Street, Hinckley,
Leicestershire LE10 3ED
Tel: 01455 631158

(Ashby Canal)
On the A5, this much modernised pub wisely turns its best side to the canal with a well-manicured garden and moorings for patrons. A good range of real ales and food is served daily, both lunchtimes and evenings.

WHARF INN
Hinckley, Leicestershire
Coventry Road, Hinckley,
Leicestershire LE10 0NQ
Tel: 01455 615830
www.wharf-inn.co.uk

(Ashby Canal)
The Wharf Inn's interior is timber-lined and cool – ideal for red hot summer days. As well as a bar and lounge, there are a number of smaller 'snug type' rooms for relaxed conversation, and a patio and garden area too.

GRAND UNION LEICESTER SECTION & RIVER SOAR

Norton Junction to Trent Junction
66 miles/59 locks/3 tunnels

The Leicester Section is vastly more attractive than its name suggests; indeed, its 20-mile summit pound is one of the loveliest stretches of canal in the country. From the top of the Watford flight of locks, the waterway ploughs a lonely furrow across the rolling Leicestershire landscape, twisting and turning, shunning all the paraphernalia of 21st century Britain, totally at ease, it seems, with its own company. Few villages venture close to the navigation, although the short Welford Arm allows the boater a brief brush with civilisation.

Foxton Locks bring an abrupt end to the isolation. The two five-rise staircases are immensely popular with gongoozlers, but perhaps less so with inexperienced boaters who sometimes struggle to cope with the complexities of staircase locking. At the foot of the locks, the Market Harborough Arm allows access to this pleasant market town.

Fine countryside accompanies the navigation (canalised river from Aylestone) all the way to Leicester. This large multi-cultural city has all the attractions and facilities – and most of the problems too – that you would expect of a major conurbation. Mooring sites here need to be chosen with great care. But Leicester does have the National Space Centre and a plethora of good Indian restaurants.

The River Soar is arguably less attractive as you head north, but Barrow-upon-Soar is a pretty village and Loughborough has much of interest for the canal traveller. Thereafter the Soar valley is compromised by electricity pylons, low flying aircraft bound for East

Midlands airport and the vast cooling towers of Ratcliffe power station as the navigation approaches Trent Junction.

THE NAVIGATION

Barrow-upon-Soar, Leicestershire

PUB FACTS

Location	87 Mill Lane, Barrow-upon-Soar, Leicestershire LE12 8LQ
Tel	01509 412842
Proprietors	Chris & Sue Lee
Manager	Neill Stevens
Opening hours	Mon–Sat 12pm–11pm, Sun 12pm–10.30pm
Food served	12pm–2.30pm
Real ales	Abbot Ale, Adnams Bitter, Fuller's London Pride, Black Sheep Best Bitter, Timothy Taylors Landlord, Star Bitter from the local Belvoir Brewery and occasional guest beers
Moorings	Outside pub or on opposite bank

In 1974, the third year of the Mikron Theatre Company's waterways touring, we spent the summer months taking a wooden ex-working boat, the *Flower of Gloster*, around the system. There were many incidents, due mainly to our incompetence or, putting it more kindly, lack of experience. I remember particularly being stuck on the edge of a weir on the River Soar when one of our crew 'blew' a bend. He took no preventative action but went catatonic, like a hedgehog in the middle of a busy road. One of our heroic band walked down the weir and went off to find the police (no mobile phones in those days). We were eventually pulled off after an hour or so by the first boat that passed.

On that day in 1974, we found a safe haven when we tied up at the Navigation,

Barrow-on-Soar, and since then it has always been one of my favourite pubs. Built in 1794 to help assuage the thirsts of boatmen and bargees, it nestles naturally alongside Bridge 28. It now has a large patio area alongside the canal, a great place to sit and watch the boats go by and to sample the wide variety of well kept real ales.

Inside, the pub has been extended from its original size, but still retains a real country pub atmosphere. When ordering the home-cooked food or a pint of Star Bitter, say – a crisp, dry, amber beer – have a look at the bar top. It's made from lots of shiny pre-decimal pennies. For a really cosy evening, go into the tiny front bar where you can eavesdrop on everyone's conversation!

The pub welcomes boaters but it also has a healthy local trade, helping it to survive in winter. Characters abound, sitting in the same seat every day and ordering the same beer. To avoid libel actions, I'll only mention some from the past: how about Jack the Strap, so-called because he was a bottle-of-whisky-a-day man who still liked a game of darts. In order for him to stand up long enough to throw his 'arrers', the landlord had fitted a strap from the ceiling at a convenient point near the ochee. So, with one hand in the strap for support, he tried for his one hundred and eighty with the other.

Or, and this is during Mikron's time of performing at the pub, what about the local policeman, a lovely fella who sold his helmets to passing foreign tourists and who, after closing time, would hide under the bridge waiting for the punters to leave, so he could nip in and have a pint or two.

You may be tempted to linger at this very inviting hostelry and, after a few pints, to use the strap (still there) to help you maintain your vertical position.

THE SWAN IN THE RUSHES

Loughborough, Leicestershire

PUB FACTS

Location	21 The Rushes, Loughborough, Leicestershire LE11 5BE
Tel	01509 217014
Website	www.tynemill.co.uk
Proprietors	Tynemill Ltd
Manager	Ian Bogie
Opening hours	Mon–Thu 11am–11pm, Fri/Sat 11am–12am, Sun 12pm–11pm
Food served	Daily 12pm–3pm, 6pm–9pm (except Sun evening)
Real ales	Castle Rock's Sheriff's Tipple and Harvest Pale, Adnams Bitter, Hop Back's Summer Lightning, plus one guest mild and five guest ales
Moorings	In Loughborough Basin

After the Soar Navigation had reached Loughborough from the Trent in 1778, the new wharf immediately became an important part of the daily life of the town – a bustling, vibrant place with all types of goods being loaded and unloaded. Business surged again in 1794 with the arrival of the Leicester Navigation and the building of a tramway to the Charnwood quarries. The shareholders were delighted to receive 150% dividends.

The wharf has recently been redeveloped. It has thirty-five apartments, two restaurants and some moorings for boats. You'll have to decide whether you love it or loathe it. A short walk from there will take you into a lively, friendly town – home of bell-making and of a university that has nurtured many a sporting hero. Sainsburys is just around the corner, if you wish, but why not go to the open market instead? But what you must do is visit the Swan in the Rushes.

Just immediately across the road from the basin, this pub, from the outside, is not particularly appealing – a typical late nineteenth century town drinking house. But venture inside and you will immediately feel at home. Turn left in the lobby and you'll be in the Green Room or Smoke Room, as is etched on the windows. Ian, the young, welcoming manager, says this is the more academic bar where a mixture of tutors from the university and office 'suits' gather. There is a newspaper rack featuring a variety of reputable daily newspapers. Turn right and you enter the Red Room or Vaults Bar, where you'll find chippies and mechanics and, oddly, tutors from the Art Department.

You may be the only boaters in the pub, but you will be immediately welcomed and information elicited about your canal journey. Don't worry which bar you're in. Some people use both and there is much good-willed banter between the two.

The atmosphere is great but this is highlighted by the wonderful range of real ales available. This is a beer drinker's paradise. There is something to suit every palate and you can even risk (if you're safely tied up in the basin, that is) trying some of the draught and bottled foreign beers. My recommendation is Duvel, meaning the Devil.

Before retiring to your bunk, why not taste one of the thirty malt whiskies.

Freshly made, healthy food is another lure: six specials on daily including the ever-present, even infamous, chilli con carne, introduced to the East Midlands in 1977 by Betty Holmes, mother of the founder of Tynemill. She was uninspired by the normal basic and boring pub fare at that time. And, as in all Tynemill pubs, there are no chips to be seen.

If you are unfortunate enough to be travelling by road, the pub offers excellent accommodation. There is also often entertainment in the upstairs functions room, be it the annual visit from Mikron, the two beer festivals, the folk club or Club Sporadic, which showcases local musical talent. You might like to hire the fold-out skittle alley for a different type of evening.

The Swan in the Rushes is one of Tynemill's twenty or so pubs, mainly in the East Midlands. The company is probably the biggest exponent of quality ale in the country and of proper pubs – no theme, no concept, no image. No large sign outside saying 'Real Alehouse'. Word of mouth does it all.

The Swan has extended itself a little recently: better toilets, larger family and function rooms, and a new terrace and beer garden, and is an even more welcoming pub than before.

OTHER PUBS WORTH TRYING

Grand Union Canal (Leicester Section) and River Soar

BRIDGE 61

Foxton, Leicestershire

Bottom Lock, Foxton, Leicestershire
LE16 7RA
Tel: 0116 279 2285

Day-trippers to the landmark lock staircase and former inclined plane at Foxton may head straight for the gleaming new Foxton Locks Inn, but the boaters' favourite is a tiny pub by the bottom lock, Bridge 61 – you'll cross the bridge to get to it – and we think the beer and cider are better here.

THE GATE HANGS WELL

Syston, Leicestershire

Lewin Bridge, Fosse Way, Syston,
Leicestershire LE7 8NH
Tel: 0116 260 9242

Actually a mile-and-a-half up the River Wreake, a very pleasant walk from the Old Junction on the Soar Navigation – boots recommended, and a torch in the evening! Ales are Leicester favourites Everards, and there's a riverside beer garden.

WATERSIDE INN

Mountsorrel, Leicestershire

Sileby Road, Mountsorrel,
Leicestershire LE12 7BB
Tel: 0116 230 2758

With a front door that opens right onto the lockside – could there be a better location? Whitewashed building and outdoor tables make a perfect pub scene, and the local Everards beer is good, too. Well-prepared pub grub and, happily, plenty of low-priced snacks.

ALBION

Loughborough, Leicestershire

Off Bridge Street, Loughborough,
Leicestershire LE11 1QA
Tel: 01509 213952

This old-fashioned 'real pub' on the canal bank serves excellent ale and, together with the Swan in the Rushes, makes Loughborough a must-visit location for the beery boater. A friendly welcome is assured in a pub run by canal enthusiasts, and mooring is easy.

STEAMBOAT INN

Trent Lock, Long Eaton, Nottinghamshire

Lock Lane, Trent Lock, Long Eaton,
Nottinghamshire NG10 2FY
Tel: 0115 946 3955

Part of British Waterways' pub chain, this pub still retains an individual atmosphere, and it's a great location – at the always busy, often chaotic junction between the Erewash Canal, River Trent and River Soar. Built by the Erewash Canal Company, it overlooks the first lock on the canal.

RIVER SEVERN

Gloucester to Stourport
42 miles/5 locks

Wild and relatively uncommercialised, the Severn is a majestic river flowing through some superb Worcestershire and Gloucestershire countryside. Its banks are somewhat high, mooring places are limited and the river is prone to flooding; none of which sounds too promising, but this navigation nevertheless offers a memorable cruising experience, as well as forming part of both the Avon and Stourport Rings.

Stourport can effectively be regarded as the upper limit of navigation. Pleasant scenery accompanies the boater down to the fine city of Worcester, whose magnificent cathedral stands photogenically beside the water. Upton-on-Severn, some ten miles downstream, is an utterly charming little town: thoroughly English, it's a place to sit by the river on a warm sunny day and then enjoy tea and cakes in a quiet tearoom. Tempted? Visitor moorings are available either side of the bridge if you are.

The Severn only skirts Tewkesbury, that noble town belonging more properly to the Avon, and then you're on the final run in to Gloucester. Here you can enjoy the fascinating docks and the superb Waterways Museum before travelling further south on the Gloucester & Sharpness Canal.

An excursion vessel on the Severn at Stourport.

BOAT INN

Ashleworth Quay, nr Gloucester, Gloucestershire

PUB FACTS

Location	Ashleworth Quay, nr Gloucester, Gloucestershire GL19 4HZ
Tel	01452 700272
Website	www.boat-inn.co.uk
Licensees	Ron, Elizabeth & Louise Nicholls
Opening hours	Tue, Thu & Fri 11.30am–2.30pm, Tue–Sat 6.30pm–11pm (Sept–Easter 7pm–11pm), Sat 11.30am–3pm, Sun 12pm–3pm, 7pm–10.30pm Closed all day Mon, and Wed lunchtime
Food served	Filled rolls and snacks (lunchtime only)
Real ales	Varied. Changes every week
Moorings	Outside pub on floating pontoon

There are six accessible riverside inns along the River Severn between Tewkesbury and Gloucester, all offering good refreshment in the way of beer and food for passing walkers, boaters and car drivers with good maps. But, for me, the jewel in the crown is, without question, the Boat Inn at Ashleworth Quay. Not the least of its distinctive qualities is that it has been run by the same family for 400 years.

The Jelf family was granted a royal charter to sell liquor after they had helped Charles II to escape from the Roundheads. And ale has been served here ever since and always by members of the Jelf family.

The land around the inn originally belonged to St Augustine's monastery in Bristol and the Abbot built the quay and a tithe barn to store and ship produce to Bristol. The tithe barn is another reason to visit the quay – an awe-inspiring building, 125 feet long and 25 feet wide with its splendid queen-post roof trusses, diagonal buttresses and transepts with curved wooden lintels.

Nowadays, if you are walking the Severn Way, you'll only be able to look longingly across the river at the Boat, tantalisingly close but unreachable. Until the 1950s, there was a ferry to whisk you across. The towpath had changed sides here and the barge horses were transported across the river. The stables and the building which was the smithy still remain at the pub today. Hay was taken from here by barge to Birmingham and coal was loaded for the return trip. The chain ferry was washed away by a flood in 1910 and replaced with a punt, run by Edward Jelf at 2d a go.

Water has always been a problem at the Boat. The heavy rains of 2007 closed the pub from July until December. There were many feet of water in the bar. Don't worry. Apart from a new elm bar, the place remains the same with its rustic furniture, kitchen range and rush mats providing a haven of conviviality.

Conversation is the order of the day. There is no piped music, no jukebox, no one-armed bandit and no dogs. Water is rarely served. But you can sample a delicious variety of real ales, constantly changing. Often there are beers from Wye Valley, RCH of Weston-super-Mare, Archers and Arkells breweries, and you must try one of the ciders or perrys. If you feel like exercise, you can always indulge in a game of shove-ha'penny, dominoes or cribbage.

The grounds of the Boat Inn are a sheer delight. There are flowers everywhere, a lovely crazy-paved courtyard and an outbuilding where, at lunchtime, you buy rolls from a local bakery, stuffed with ham from a local butcher or cheese with chutney, made by the family from a secret recipe.

Long may this most unique pub survive as it is today – a classic example of what English pubs used to be about before the corporate onslaught and the arrival of the ubiquitous chip.

Go there tomorrow.

Ashleworth Tithe Barn
Open to the public April–October

CAMP HOUSE INN

Grimley, Worcester

PUB FACTS

Location	Camp Lane, Grimley, Worcester, Worcestershire WR2 6LX
Tel	01905 640288
Lessees	Jim & Lynne Wainwright
Opening hours	12pm–11pm every day
Food served	12pm–2pm, 6pm–8pm
Real ales	Flowers IPA, Batham's Best Bitter, Old Speckled Hen and a real cider, Thatchers Medium
Moorings	Landing stage below pub. Also facilities for caravans and tents

If you journey down the River Severn from Stourport towards Worcester, you will pass through Lincombe and Holt locks and then, not long afterwards, you arrive at Bevere Lock. A loop in the river forms the island of Bevere, a place that the people of Worcester should have a soft spot for. It has been a refuge for them when they were fleeing the Danes in 1031, and again in 1637, when a lucky few escaped the ravages of the Plague by isolating themselves here.

Just below the lock is the site of another refuge – the Camp House Inn. It was to here that the Royalists fled in 1651 after the Battle of Worcester. Charlie's (later the Second) boys had been given a right old thumping by Cromwell. They hid here and then retreated to a farm up the hill (today called Retreat Farm).

A refuge for them and a refuge for us today. An escape from the hustle and bustle of our everyday lives. The Camp House is a magnificent building of mixed parentage. Possibly the tower piece survives from the Civil War days, when it would have been used as a lookout over the river. A lot of it is Georgian. The indoor toilets are 1980. The garden running down to the river is dominated by a very large, very old, horse chestnut tree, described by those who know as the finest tree in Worcestershire. You'll see (and hear!) peacocks, and a wonderful array of bantams and chickens wander around.

It is not just the history, the building and its surroundings that make this place special. It's the people who run it. Jim was born in the pub, which his parents started running in 1939.

Jim and his wife, Lynne, took over in 1971 and, 37 years later, they're still at it. There are campers, caravanners and boaters in the summer, and a regular car trade (despite the Camp House being quite difficult to find), with 'the retirees with a bit of income' keeping them going in the winter.

Lynne makes most of the food herself – pheasant casserole, steak pies with big chunks of meat, vegetable lasagne and chilli. The jumbo sausages and burgers come from a Black Country butcher. I can also personally recommend the scrumpy. Delicious - but treat it with respect. It's 6%.

The River Severn itself also has to be treated with respect, as Jim and Lynne know only all too well. Every winter the pub floods but, in the summer of 2007, they were closed for three weeks. The water in the pub was over waist high. It's just part of living there. You listen to the weather forecast and, if it's very heavy rain in Wales, you start moving all the furniture out of the pub.

So, it takes a certain type of person to put up with the traumas of flooding in return for living and working in a idyllic setting. Jim and Lynne take it in their stride and continue to run a wonderful pub.

OTHER PUBS WORTH TRYING

River Severn

MUG HOUSE

Bewdley, Worcestershire
12 Severnside North, Bewdley,
Worcestershire DY12 2EE
Tel: 01299 402543
www.mughousebewdley.co.uk

Narrowboats and cruisers don't reach as far upstream as Bewdley, but the river here is still wide and busy with rowers, and this is a good vantage point. A traditional pub (real ale and cider) with an adventurous restaurant, and a charming warren of a B&B, all winding staircases and low roof beams. It can get very busy at weekends, and deservedly so.

YE OLDE CROWN INN

Stourport, Worcestershire
9 Bridge Street, Stourport-on-
Severn, Worcestershire DY13 8XB
Tel: 01299 825693

A Wetherspoons pub-by-numbers might seem a little out of place in this book, but this one scores for its great location – right next to the imposing Stourport Bridge, with a very pleasant outside balcony. The usual wide range of real ale and cider, and cheap food.

ANGEL INN

Stourport, Worcestershire
Severn Side, Stourport-on-Severn,
Worcestershire DY13 9EW
Tel: 01299 822661

An outstanding, historic red-brick pub on the river, just downstream of the canal entrance. Good Banks's beer and excellent real cider; take your pick between the characteristically Midland interior with friendly locals, or the plentiful outside seating. Worth seeking out.

KINGS HEAD

Upton, Worcestershire
Riverside, Upton-on-Severn,
Worcestershire WR8 0HF
Tel: 01684 592621
www.kingsheadupton.co.uk

One of the most delightful stop-offs on the Severn, with its distinctive cupola, independent shops and music festivals. This pub is right at the heart of the community, with frequent live music, while the river terrace makes the most of its position. Food and ales are traditional British and all the better for it.

COAL HOUSE INN

Apperley, Gloucestershire
Gabb Lane, Apperley,
Gloucestershire GH9 4DN
Tel: 01452 780211

A friendly, secluded pub, this little inn is a pleasant change from the cavernous pubs often found by rivers. The 300 year old building was once used for coal distribution along the Severn. Now, it serves real ale and the speciality 'Steak on a Stone'.

SHROPSHIRE UNION CANAL

Autherley Junction (Wolverhampton) to Ellesmere Port
66.5 miles/47 locks/1 tunnel

An integral part of the popular Four Counties Ring, the Shropshire Union Canal is a bold and decisive beast, striding powerfully across the landscape on high embankments and through deep cuttings, in a powerful hurry to get from Wolverhampton to Ellesmere Port. Not that it lacks charm, for its journey takes it through a host of inviting towns and villages, and through a delectable landscape comparatively little changed by the march of time.

Highlights of this super canal are numerous enough to make selection difficult. There's Brewood, so close to Wolverhampton but so villagey; the impressive cutting at Woodseaves; Market Drayton, with its ancient market and statue of Robert Clive; the pretty lock flights at Adderley and Audlem; the busy junctions at Hurleston and Barbridge; and, of course, Nantwich, beautified by its floral displays and its black and white architecture.

The nature of the canal changes north of Nantwich, becoming wider, more winding and with broad locks. At Barbridge the Middlewich Arm provides a link with the Trent & Mersey Canal. On the Main Line several miles of pleasant cruising bring you to the fabulous city of Chester, with attractions too numerous to detail here. (But do find the time to walk the City Walls and visit the Deeside Promenade.) Many boaters end their exploration of the Shroppie here, but it's certainly worth proceeding past Chester Zoo and on to Ellesmere Port, if only to visit the Boat Museum or to gaze at the wide waters of the Manchester Ship Canal and the Mersey beyond.

Tyrley Wharf and Top Lock near Market Drayton.

THE ANCHOR INN

High Offley, Staffordshire

PUB FACTS

Location	Peggs Lane, Old Lea, High Offley, Staffordshire ST20 ONG
Tel	01785 284569
Proprietors	Olive & Elaine Cliffe
Opening hours	Summer: 12pm–3pm, 7pm–11pm End of October until Easter: Fri 7pm–11pm, Sat 12pm–3pm, 7pm–11pm, Sun 12pm–3pm
Food served	Sandwiches and toasties (anytime when open)
Real ales	Wadworth 6X
Moorings	Outside pub and along towpath Also facilities for caravans and tents

The Anchor Inn has not changed on the outside since it was built in about 1826. It was a boat people's pub known as both the Sebastopol (after the nearby bridge, which took its name from the famous siege in the Crimean War) and the New Inn. No one is quite sure when it became the Anchor Inn.

The interior has also changed very little. The tiny main bar has a tiled floor, well-scrubbed wooden bench seating, and high-backed settles and a little coal fire. The small servery looks like the side of a boat and there are other canal objects, including a Buckby can and butty tiller, both painted by the artist, Tony Lewery, and photographs. There is also a grandfather clock, made between 1826-30. It has roses and castles as part of its decoration. These designs, fashionable at the time, were used by the boat people to decorate their boats. The other room (also tiny) is the 'modernised' part of the pub. It was decorated in the 1960s.

The landlady for many years was Lily Pascall. When her husband died, she carried on running the pub until shortly before her death in 1970, at the age of 89. She is remembered as a real character who went up and down the cellar steps in her wellies to bring the beer to her customers in a jug. Her nephew, Graham, took over the pub and ran it with his wife, Olive, until his very untimely death in 1986.

Little did Olive realise that she was going to follow in Lily's footsteps and run a pub. But, as she says, it had to be done: "Nobody else wanted it". Fortunately, she has a daughter, Elaine, who is as potty as she is and they've been running the pub together ever since.

Nothing has really changed since Lily's day: the beer is still fetched in a jug from the cellar (although there are now also many types of cider and perry available on draught or in bottles), the toilets are still outside and the only music you hear is if a group of folk musicians turns up for the evening and out come the fiddles and bodhrans. Most unusually for pub landlords, Olive and Elaine are both teetotal. Often to be seen with a

cup of tea, they've never tried their delicious 6X or any other alcohol: "Best not to when you're running a pub".

Elaine has transformed the garden. There are flowers everywhere and she has been winning first prizes in the Stafford garden competitions since 2002. She also runs a well-stocked gift shop at the rear of the pub.

The other change since Lily's day is that more and more people come by road to seek out the tranquility of the Anchor, some of them complete with tents and caravans. But it's never what you might call overcrowded. Mainly because it's not everyone's cup of tea – no theme, no hot food, no jukebox and no children's climbing frame. But also it's pretty hard to find in a car along windy single-track roads. I think it becomes a bit of a challenge. But once found, you'll keep coming back.

THE BOAT INN

Gnosall, Staffordshire

PUB FACTS

Location	Wharf Road, Gnosall, Staffordshire ST20 0DA
Tel	01785 822208
Email	neil@atkinson7.orangehome.co.uk
Lessee	Neil Atkinson
Opening hours	Sun–Thu 12pm–12am, Fri/Sat 12pm–1am
Food served	12pm–2.30pm (Sun 4pm), 6pm–8.30pm (except Sun – free supper with quiz)
Real ales	Banks's Original, Banks's Bitter, Marston's Burton Bitter, Marston's Pedigree and regular guest beers
Real ciders	Bulmer's Medium and Dry, plus several other keg ciders
Moorings	Outside pub and on towpath opposite

The Shropshire Union Canal, or Shroppie, opened between Nantwich and Autherley in 1835 as the Birmingham & Liverpool Junction Canal. At about the same time, the cottage or cottages adjoining bridge number 34 were converted into a pub, with stabling for boat horses underneath. The stables have long gone, but the pub is still very distinctive with an intriguing bay window overlooking the canal and a curved wall abutting the bridge.

Sit in the seats in the bay window at your peril. Neil, the landlord, says the locals would like it roped off. But, instead, there is a prominent sign which says: 'The OG and PA Corner'. OG can mean 'older gentlepersons' or 'old gits' and PA can be interpreted as 'physically afflicted' or some type of 'artist'. The sign continues: "Please note that this area is reserved for members only. Non-members will be overcharged and asked to leave this area (or made to stay and have a conversation with the members which could be even worse!)".

There are canal photos and paintings and Buckby cans alongside the pool table, darts board, juke box and games machine. Strangely, there is also an upside-down canoe suspended from the ceiling. It's a pub where you feel compelled to join in either with one of the intense conversations being held by the bar huggers or in one of the games. Not surprisingly, there are five darts teams, a dominoes team and a pool team.

It's a beer pub with excellent Banks's and Marston's beers but also an interesting variety of guest beers, including Dark Destroyer, Cocker Hoop, Old Hooky, Owd Roger, Nosy Rosy and Wicked Witch.

But your appetite can also be satisfied with good pub grub, including steaks, pizzas, home-made casseroles and liver and onions, as well as light snacks and starters and desserts. Neil says he is lucky to have such a wonderful butcher just across the road. Wily boaters know to stock up here. Try wandering further afield into Gnosall itself, where there is a local bakery and a great greengrocer.

Go back to the pub with your shopping and, if it's a sunny day, sit on the patio outside and boat watch or, if it's a Sunday evening, join in the pub quiz and earn your free supper. About fifty people do so every week. They pay £1 to enter but there's a first and second prize and a booby prize for the lowest score. Don't try not answering the questions to win this as, although sometimes it could be a jug of beer, it's as likely to be a packet of crisps or the opportunity to clean the pub after closing time.

OTHER PUBS WORTH TRYING

Shropshire Union Canal

BUNBURY ARMS

Stoak, Cheshire
Little Stanney Lane, Stoak,
Cheshire CH2 4HW
Tel: 01244 301665

Despite its proximity to Ellesmere Port and the M56, this feels very much like a country pub with a cosy, relaxed atmosphere. A former CAMRA 'Summer Pub of the Year', it has a good selection of cask ales and its food is well renowned locally.

TELFORD'S WAREHOUSE

Chester
Canal Basin, Tower Wharf,
Chester CH1 4EZ
Tel: 01244 390090
www.telfordswarehouse.com

This Grade 2 listed building converted into a pub in the 1980s, is an immensely popular bar/restaurant and thriving music and arts venue. A large selection of European beers, CAMRA rated cask ales and extensive wine list. Imaginative restaurant menu and friendly attentive service.

OLDE BARBRIDGE INN

Barbridge, Cheshire
Old Chester Road, Barbridge,
Cheshire CW5 6AY
Tel: 01270 528443
www.the-olde-barbridge-inn.co.uk

With canalside moorings, a 40-seat restaurant, lounge, public bar and games room, as well as a pleasant garden with children's play area, this pub is understandably one of the most popular ports of call on the northern Shroppie. There's a wide – and alternating – range of cask ales on offer too.

SHROPPIE FLY

Audlem, Chesire
The Wharf, Shropshire Street,
Audlem, Cheshire CW3 0DX
Tel: 01270 811772
www.shroppiefly.co.uk

Originally a canal warehouse dating back to the construction of the Shropshire Union, this friendly pub has a large canalside beer garden. Good food is served daily, and there is a well-established calendar of live music. Real ales available.

HARTLEY ARMS

Wheaton Aston, Staffordshire
56 Long Street, Wheaton Aston,
Staffordshire ST19 9NF
Tel: 01785 840232

Close to Wheaton Aston Lock, a popular boaters' pub, with customer moorings. There's a pleasant outside seating area, good choice of beers and food both lunchtimes and evenings; the carvery is especially well regarded.

Staffs & Worcs Canal

Great Haywood to Stourport-on-Severn
46 miles/43 locks/1 tunnel

An extremely popular canal, the Staffs & Worcs was built to link the Trent & Mersey Canal with the River Severn at Stourport. It is a fascinatingly varied waterway which, despite straying precariously close to the Black Country, succeeds in protecting its rural identity throughout.

Great Haywood, complete with boatyard and graceful towpath bridge, is one of the loveliest canal junctions on the system. Tixall Wide – thought to have been created to enhance the view from Tixall Hall – maintains the beauty, as does the passage past Milford, where there are fine views of Cannock Chase to the south.

Beyond Penkridge – a lively town where shopping remains a pleasure – the canal skirts around the outskirts of Wolverhampton. Two junctions follow in quick succession: Autherley, where the Shropshire Union Canal heads off to the north, and Aldersley, from where you can join the BCN.

Bratch Locks are extremely photogenic, and extremely congested in high summer. Not quite a staircase, this flight of three locks features very short pounds between each chamber. Chaotic scenes occasionally occur in high summer, as inexperienced boaters panic and start opening paddles all over the shop, but a lockkeeper is normally on hand to restore a measure of equilibrium.

Continuing its descent towards the Severn, the Staffs & Worcs keeps itself to itself, diving through deep cuttings and snaking through rich woodlands. Only Kidderminster interrupts the rural idyll. Stourport – an interesting town with some

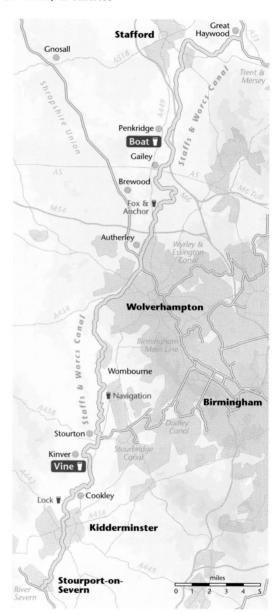

fine architecture and a series of connected basins – marks journey's end for this delightful canal.

THE BOAT

Penkridge, Staffordshire

PUB FACTS

Location	Cannock Road, Penkridge, Staffordshire ST19 5DT
Tel	01785 714178
Email	chriswhitehouse@btinternet.com
Website	www.theboatatpenkridge.co.uk
Lessee	Chris Whitehouse
Opening hours	Mon–Sat 11am–12am, Sun 12pm–11pm
Food served	Mon–Fri 12pm–9pm, Sat 12pm–10pm, Sun 12pm–8pm
Real ales	Greene King's Abbot Ale plus a changing guest beer, eg. Wells Bombardier, Courage Directors Bitter
Moorings	Outside pub

There is one peculiarity about the Boat at Penkridge. It is the pub sign. The Boat is situated just below Penkridge Lock on the north Staffordshire & Worcestershire Canal. It was part of James Brindley's idea to build a Grand Cross of canals linking the Thames, Trent, Severn and Mersey. It was the only one of his canals that James

THE BOAT

way to and from Littleton Colliery (closed in 1992) and provided the changing rooms for Penkridge United football team. It was also a mecca of entertainment with concerts, conjurors and comedians.

Brindley lived to see opened throughout. And, from 1772 until the 1950s, it was a very successful commercial waterway. The last traffic was coal being moved by a fleet of 70 pairs of narrowboats from the Cannock area to Stourport power station. So why is the painting on the pub sign that of a very large tanker going along what could be the Aire & Calder Navigation? I'd be delighted to know the answer to this mystery.

In fact, the building was there before the canal. It was built as a mill house in 1711. It became an ale house in 1779 and catered for the many boat people passing through.

The whole area became busy with a wharf, warehouses and cottages, and the pub would have provided sustenance for the workers and for people arriving along the turnpike road from Cannock. It had to provide a bed for the night, simple victuals and stabling.

In the twentieth century, the Boat became a gathering point for local men on their

The Boat is attractively laid out with many black and white photos of narrowboats at work (not one of a tanker!), tiled floors, bench seats, a real fire in the restaurant and a beautiful range made by Harlows of Burton-on-Trent in the bar. The beers are good and the guest ale changes regularly, and the freshly made food offers something for everyone. There's a lunch menu (how about a Boat Burger Classic for £3.95?), an evening menu, a Sunday roast at £6.95 and a children's menu. There are plenty of tables outside overlooking the canal where the gongoozlers can watch the boats negotiating their way into the lock.

You may be walking the Staffordshire Way, which uses the canal towpath between bridges 90 and 86 and in several other places, as it makes its way from Mow Kop to Kinver Edge. You may be on a boat enjoying the scenery of the Staffs & Worcs as you lock your way towards Cannock Chase. You may be out walking your dog. You'll all be made welcome by the young, friendly staff at the Boat and that definitely includes the dog. And don't forget to have a look at the sign.

THE VINE

Kinver, Stourbridge, West Midlands

PUB FACTS

Location	1 Dunsley Road, Kinver, Stourbridge, West Midlands DY7 6L
Tel	01384 877291
Website	www.vineinnkinver.co.uk
Lessees	Craig Brown & Bill Kendrick
Opening hours	12pm–11pm
Food served	12pm–2.15pm, 6pm–9.15pm (£4.25–£14.95)
Real ales	Kinver Edge
Moorings	Below Kinver Lock

The Staffs & Worcs is one my favourite canals, alongside such as the Leeds & Liverpool and the Caldon. It is a classic example of an early narrow waterway as it twists and turns its 46 miles from the Trent & Mersey at Great Haywood to the River Severn at Stourport. It is always interesting but never less so than in the area of Kidderminster and Kinver with its deep narrow cuttings through the red sandstone, exemplified by the huge overhang at Austcliff.

So, after such exertions, even more reason to stop off for a pint or two and some good food at a canalside pub. You will do no better than to tie up below Kinver Lock and wander up to the Vine.

We must all thank Henry Hicks, a local coal merchant and boat owner, who opened one of the Georgian cottages alongside the canal as a beer shop in 1863 to compete with the Lock Inn opposite, a fully licensed ale house which dated from the time in the late eighteenth century when the canal was being built. The Vine wasn't given full alehouse status until 1951. The Lock Inn and the adjoining wharf have

long since disappeared but the Vine goes from strength to strength and is, deservedly, a very popular canalside pub used by boaters, walkers, bikers and locals alike. Oh, and if you insist, it does, of course, have a road leading to it!

The pub boasts a very large canalside garden with planted areas and umbrellas. The decking at the lock side of the pub extends right round the back and the little listed weighhouse and its weighbridge, which were part of the old coal wharf, have been restored, again linking the pub to its past.

Kinver Edge is a beautifully hoppy beer from the local brewery and in the restaurant, which overlooks the lock, I can recommend the Chef's Bruschetta with its tomato, bacon and mozzarella as a starter (£4.25) and why not follow that with lamb shank on a bed of mash with fresh vegetables (£10.95). All the food is freshly cooked and locally sourced. There are always daily specials and they often have a theme night such as French, Italian or Mediterranean.

Kinver Edge itself is a must see. It's an ancient sandstone ridge with wonderful heathland to wander about in. Watch out for adders! You must also explore the many rock houses which many years ago were gouged out of the rock. They were all lived in until the 1960s and recently the National Trust has restored two of them. One is again lived in, the other shows what life would have been like in the early twentieth century, with its fireplace and plastered and painted walls.

Then it's back to the Vine for a refreshing pint and another nod of thanks to Henry Hicks. I think he would be delighted to know that his weighhouse lives on and that the pub has an assured future.

OTHER PUBS WORTH TRYING
Staffs & Worcs Canal

NAVIGATION INN

Greensforge, West Midlands
Greensforge, Kingswinford, West
Midlands DY6 0AH
Tel: 01384 273721

Situated above the lock on one of the prettiest stretches of the Staffs & Worcs Canal, this pub is popular with boaters and motorists alike – the latter come in droves on summer weekends to observe the activity on the canal. Food is served daily and real ale is on offer too.

THE LOCK

Wolverley, Worcestershire
Wolverley Road, Wolverley,
Kidderminster DY10 3RN
Tel: 01562 850581

Overlooking Wolverley Lock – as the name suggests – this pub attracts plenty of punters out from Kidderminster, just a couple of miles away by road. Boaters, too, enjoy its lockside garden and cool, cosy interior. There is a good selection of beers, and reasonably priced, very filling food is served lunchtimes and evenings.

FOX & ANCHOR

Coven, Wolverhapton
Brewood Road, Coven,
Wolverhampton WV9 5BX
Tel: 01902 798786

The beer garden here almost spills out onto the narrow towpath, making it a great place to sit on a summer afternoon. Part of the Vintage Inns chain, it nonetheless has respectable pub grub and real ales, making it a popular overnighting place for passing boaters. Easy to get to, it's just off the A449.

STRATFORD UPON AVON CANAL

Kings Norton Junction to Stratford
25 miles/54 locks/1 tunnel

While the best way to arrive in Stratford is via the River Avon, the Stratford Canal is a close runner up. Heavily locked, the waterway is always pleasantly rural, with some beautiful sections south of Kingswood Junction.

Leaving the Worcester & Birmingham Canal at Kings Norton Junction, the canal passes through the guillotine gated stop lock and strides off to the south, in a hurry, it seems, to free itself of Birmingham's cloying presence. Locks come thick and fast as the canal descends to Lapworth, where Kingswood Junction – a pretty parting of the ways – offers access to the Grand Union Canal.

The southern section of the Stratford Canal is beguilingly lovely. There are so many highlights: timber-framed Packwood Hall, just a short walk from Lapworth; the distinctive barrel-roofed lock cottages; the elegant iron aqueducts at Wootton Wawen and Edstone; and not least miles of wonderfully unspoilt Warwickshire countryside, little visited by the tourist masses who descend on Stratford throughout the year.

The Shakespeare connection comes to the fore at Wilmcote, Mary Arden's cottage (open to the public) is just a short distance from the canal. The final approach to Stratford, is surprisingly industrial. But soon enough you pass under a road bridge and enter the pretty canal basin, with all the glories of this major tourist destination at your disposal. So too is the River Avon, reached by a single lock.

A typical Stratford Canal split bridge near Preston Bagot.

FLEUR DE LYS

Lowsonford, Henley-in-Arden, Warwickshire

PUB FACTS

Location	Lapworth Street, Lowsonford, Henley-in-Arden, Warwickshire B95 5HJ
Tel	01564 782431
Email	pete.graham1@btinternet.com
Website	www.fleur-de-lys-lowsonford.com
Tenants	Pete, Gail & Matt Graham
Opening hours	Mon–Sat 11am–11pm, Sun 12pm–11pm
Food served	Mon–Sat 12pm–10pm, Sun 12pm–9.30pm (Prices from £3.25–£14.95)
Real ales	Greene King IPA, Abbot Ale and a guest beer
Moorings	Outside pub and on towpath side opposite

I'm a Midlands lad – born and brought up in Coventry. Although I moved away when I was eighteen, you never really escape, do you? As you get to a certain age, memories of your youth come flooding back. Often, in the summer, I went with my parents to a pub called, rather mysteriously, the Fleur de Lys.

Why did we travel all the way from Coventry to the pretty little village of Lowsonford? To sample the mouth-watering Fleur de Lys pies baked on the premises. It was the only place you could get them and people queued for hours for a taste of steak and kidney or chicken and mushroom. They melted in your mouth. By the late 1950s, the production of the pies moved to a factory in Leamington. The romance faded and those pies never tasted as good again.

The pub was originally very small and part of a row of cottages with a blacksmith's shop at the top end. Gradually, over the years, the pub enlarged and now includes all the cottages and the blacksmith's shop. So, now one room leads into another. There are low beams, leaded windows and heaps of brass and copper. The old blacksmith's shop has scrubbed wooden tables, rugs and sofas.

The pub caters for all. Villagers pop in for a pint, but the main trade comes from visitors from Solihull and surrounding areas and from boaters in the summer. Nearby is Lock 31

with one of the tiny, characteristic barrel-shaped lock cottages alongside. Old Ned used to live there until about two years ago. Now it's a holiday cottage.

There's good beer to be had at the pub and they serve a wide variety of food, with an excellent wine list. But the best news of all is that they have revived the Fleur de Lys home-cooked pies. There are now eight different varieties.

The atmosphere of the Fleur de Lys (flower of the lily, to you), despite its modern chic style, has a calm timelessness about it. But every so often… you see, it **is** haunted – bigtime. I am assured that many of the staff and customers have heard people saying "hello" outside the Ladies toilet when there was no-one there; have heard voices coming out of the speakers; seen chairs and plates move; and have seen an old lady sitting on a sofa, who disappears when you walk towards her. The landlord watched a door moving backwards and forwards for half an hour. He didn't dare move. Probably because, a few days before, he had had spirits floating above his bed!

There's a lot of history to these buildings. Many people have lived and died there over the centuries. Don't let that put you off. Eat and drink well. Linger a little and feel the vibes. And don't forget to try the pies.

BLUE BELL CIDER HOUSE

Hockley Heath, Solihull, West Midlands

PUB FACTS

Location	Warings Green Road, Hockley Heath, Solihull, West Midlands B94 6BP
Tel	01564 702328
General Managers	Keith & Ruth Jones
Opening	Mon–Sat 11.30am–11pm, Sun 12pm–10.30pm
Food served	Mon–Sat 12pm–3pm, 6pm–9pm (except Mon eve), Sun lunch 12pm–5pm (Three meat carvery £6)
Real ales	Three guests beers, eg. Oakleaf's Maypole Mild, Deuchars IPA, & Marston's Pedigree
Real ciders	Bulmer's Medium and Dry, plus several other keg ciders
Moorings	Outside pub and on the opposite towpath side

The northern section of the North Stratford Canal is free of locks. If you're boating, you meander mostly through the semi-rural suburbs of Warstock, Shirley and Dickens Heath but there are times when you feel as if you are in a tree-enclosed wonderland of your own. Watch out for Bridge 19, for there is something to drag you from your sylvan reverie.

Perched above you on the bank is the Blue Bell Cider House, a most remarkable collection of buildings. Take a closer look from the large canalside garden. You can see the place has gone through several metamorphoses. The original cottage, probably built in the early eighteenth century, is at the core. This was extended in about 1780 into a farmhouse and pub. The outbuildings consisted of a large milking parlour for the pedigree Jersey cows, with a grain store above, and a brewery. The milking parlour is now the kitchen and toilets but the brewery building remains; alas, you won't get a waft of hops or barley. There is no longer any brewing on the premises.

The pub used to be famous for its beer – a secret recipe with low sugar content. The local farmers loved it. They drank it in large quantities from glazed jugs, probably to hide the fact that the beer was always very cloudy. It was also shipped in barrels around the country, as it was a particularly suitable beverage for diabetics.

The farm and pub were run by the Lucas family for over one hundred years. I have tried to trace a family link, but the only one I've found is that I like beer! When Mrs Lucas died in 1967, she was ninety-four years old, still serving pints and the oldest landlady in Europe, so they say. She had four sons who ran the farm and the brewery. She was in charge of the pub and you only played billiards if you were invited into the smart Billiards Room by her.

Bulmers bought the building in 1968 and it became a cider house and, although they only ran it for two years, a cider house it remains. Try the excellent range, but don't miss out on the pub's real ales. The food's pretty good too – all home-cooked and quite traditional with such delicacies as faggots and peas and liver and onions.

It's a proper pub. These places need to be championed and savoured. Beware their slow erosion and replacement with 'plastic pubs'. The Blue Bell, for example, has several rooms including a traditional public bar with a wooden floor, where the farmer or the enthusiast can drink happily together having left their respective tractor, bike or boat outside and brought their muddy boots in. There's a conservatory, added in the early 1980s, where granny and grandchildren can gather for an incredible value Sunday lunch. There's no jukebox, just conversation. There are darts teams and quiz nights, roaring fires in winter and trad jazz and pig roasts in the garden in the summer.

The pub seems remote when you're there but it's only two miles from Hockley Heath, five miles from Solihull and Henley-in-Arden and eight miles from Stratford. The regulars obviously like it. Keith, who manages this free house with his wife, Ruth, says that many of them drive past five pubs on their way to the Blue Bell. Mrs Lucas would have approved of their taste and would have certainly let them play billiards.

OTHER PUBS WORTH TRYING

Stratford upon Avon Canal

WHARF TAVERN

Hockley Heath, West Midlands
Stratford Road, Hockley Heath, West
Midlands B94 6QT
Tel: 01564 782075

Its location at a busy road crossing means the
Wharf is always busy, but the canalside aspect is
nonetheless picture-perfect – the wharf itself is
still there, overlooked by the beer garden, and the
moorings are almost always full. The real ale and
pub grub are both up to scratch.

BOOT INN

Lapworth, Warwickshire
Old Warwick Road, Lapworth,
Warwickshire B94 6JU
Tel: 01564 782464
www.bootinnlapworth.co.uk

There are nice canalside pubs, very nice canalside
pubs...and then there's the Boot at Lapworth.
Magically situated in the lush Warwickshire
countryside through which the Stratford Canal
wends its charming way, this hostelry has it all:
relaxed atmosphere, good range of ales and a
wonderful menu. Fill your boots! Forgive the pun.

THE NAVIGATION

Wootton Wawen, Warwickshire
Stratford Road, Wootton Wawen,
Warwickshire B95 6BZ
Tel: 01564 792676
www.the-navigationinn.co.uk

Dating back some 200 years, this country pub and
restaurant stands beside the aqueduct carrying
the canal over the A3400. With its large canalside
garden, it's popular with boaters and car-borne
families. There's occasional live music and trad jazz
nights, plus bar and restaurant meals. Wootton
Wawen itself is a very pleasant little village with a
Saxon church and good general stores.

WORCESTER & BIRMINGHAM CANAL

Worcester to Birmingham
30 miles/58 locks/5 tunnels

Ascending 58 locks in just 30 miles, this is one of the most heavily locked canals in the country. But it's a popular route, being part of the Avon Ring, and it traverses some pleasing, if unexceptional, countryside.

Worcester is a fine city that sadly doesn't show its best face to the canal. Diglis Basin, where the two worlds of narrowboats and seagoing craft collide, is an enjoyably atmospheric place, but thereafter the canal trudges wearily through some dreary suburbs before finally reaching open country.

The 36 locks of the Tardebigge and neighbouring Stoke flights represent a stiff challenge, but the rolling Worcestershire landscape – with distant views of the Malvern Hills – provides ample compensation for the toil.

Beyond Alvechurch – a busy boating centre – you soon reach Wast Hill Tunnel, all 2,726 yards of it. Emerging from the northern portal, you're firmly ensconced in the Birmingham conurbation. At Kings Norton Junction the Stratford Canal departs with a cheery wave, as you proceed past Bournville (where Cadbury World is a tempting port of call), through Edgbaston and on to the canal's meeting with the BCN at Gas Street Basin.

Approaching Astwood Locks on the Worcester & Birmingham Canal.

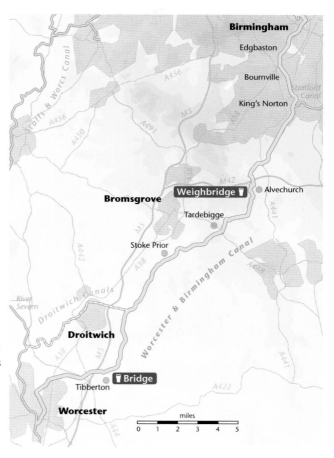

THE BRIDGE

Tibberton, Droitwich, Worcestershire

PUB FACTS

Location	Location Plough Road, Tibberton, Droitwich, Worcestershire WR9 7NQ
Tel	01905 345874
Lessee	Darren Magor
Opening hours	Mon–Fri 11.30am–3pm, 5pm–11pm, Sat 11.30am–11pm, Sun 12pm–11pm
Food served	Mon–Fri 12pm–2pm, 6pm–9pm, Sat/Sun 12pm–9pm (Prices from £3.25–£14)
Real ales	Banks's Bitter, Banks's Original, Marston's Pedigree plus a guest beer, eg. Jennings Bitter, Camerons Bitter
Moorings	Outside the pub

The Worcester & Birmingham has two fine eponymous cities at either end of it and some remote-feeling countryside, although the railway and motorway are never far away. It boasts five tunnels of varying lengths. But its real claim to fame is that it has the largest narrow canal lock flight in the country – Tardebigge. Its thirty locks raise the canal over 200 feet and its top lock – at 14 feet – is, allegedly, the deepest narrow lock on the canal system.

The Worcester & Birmingham is 30 miles long with 58 locks in all. It took 21 years to build and finally opened in 1815. At the same time, canalside pubs were being built to service the thirsts of navvies and then boatmen. One of these was the Bridge at Tibberton, a small village four miles from Worcester and Droitwich.

The pub was owned by the Tandy family for several generations. It was the sort of pub where you could wander in, order a pint and, in a few minutes, be treated like a local. The bar had a bow window where the regulars would sit and discuss the issues of the day. Although you could buy sandwiches, I distinctly remember the old men who would sit and cut up a loaf, slice thick wodges of ham and onion and make the chunkiest sarnies you'd ever seen.

The old men have long gone and the pub has been extended inside and out, but the bar is still there with its photos of old Tibberton adorning the walls. There's no jukebox and the darts board is now in a sensible position. You used to have to move half the customers in order to throw your arrers. By the way, they are looking for a new darts team. The old one resigned after constantly winning the wooden spoon in the league!

The pub now has a dining room. This has a rustic feel with exposed brick fireplace, panelled walls and photos of local interest.

The main menu features beer battered cod and honey and mustard glazed free-range chicken breasts. The Specials Board changes weekly; so you might be there for medallions of monkfish wrapped in smoked bacon served on ratatouille or mussels cooked with leeks, bacon, white wine and cream.

Boaters are particularly welcome. If you're travelling downhill, it's the last pub before Worcester. There are excellent moorings and a canalside garden, built where once were stables for the horses of Cadbury's boats, resting up on their way from Tolladine in Worcester to Bourneville. If you get stuck in a lock or on a low pound and are likely to miss last orders for food, they'll sort you out if they can at the pub, particularly if you phone and let them know.

What they probably would no longer appreciate is you taking your own bread, ham and onions into the pub. It's a shame, but times have changed. On the other hand, if you're good at darts, they may never let you leave.

THE WEIGHBRIDGE

Alvechurch, Worcestershire

PUB FACTS

Location	Scarfield Wharf, Scarfield Hill, Alvechurch, Worcestershire B48 7SQ
Tel	0121 445 5111
Website	www.the-weighbridge.co.uk
Licensees & Managers	John & Jayne Humphreys
Opening hours	12pm–3pm, 7pm–11pm (Sun 10.30pm)
Food served	12pm–2pm, 7pm–9pm
Real ales	Weatheroak's Tillerman's Tipple plus two changing guest beers
Moorings	On towpath side opposite the boatyard

When the Worcester & Birmingham opened in 1815, small industries began to grow up alongside the canal. One of them was at Scarfield Wharf (just by Bridge 60 on the canal). Here a substantial coal yard developed. There was a weighbridge for weighing the coal that was being transferred from narrowboats on to carts for local delivery by horse. A simple but elegant house was built nearby for the coal merchant.

The wharf continued in business until the 1960s. At that time, it was owned by Samuel Dedicoat who managed to combine coal deliveries with landscape gardening. In the early 70s, the house became the clubhouse for the marina, which was now established on the wharf. In 2002, the clubhouse became a pub with the very appropriate name of the Weighbridge.

It's a charming place, tucked next to the bridge and difficult to spot from the canal. It has three small rooms, one with a bar and one with a serving hatch. There's a mix of antiques, curios and boating paraphernalia. There's a covered patio, a lovely enclosed garden by the pub and a grassy area with tables down by the canal near to the famous A-framed shop of the boatyard.

There is a friendly, intimate atmosphere helped along by John, the licensee, who is as likely to fetch you a dozen free-range eggs as he is to sell you a pint. The beer is beautifully kept. The regular ale is Tillerman's Tipple, at a gentle 3.9%, made specially for the pub by Weatheroak Brewery in Alvechurch. I can personally vouch for its tastiness. There is also a guest beer. "As fast as the customers can drink it, I'll change it," says John. You might be able to sample Swillmore Original from Slaughterhouse Brewery in Warwick, Three Shires Bitter from Millstones Brewery in Mossley, Archers Golden from Swindon and many others.

The Weighbridge holds regular beer festivals in June and September, when you can sample over 30 beers and 4 ciders and perrys. Its reputation for its beers is spreading far and wide, but so is the one for its food. Jayne does all the cooking and the menu changes daily. Try the Double Decker Steak & Onion sandwich with a bowl of fries, lasagne, spaghetti Bolognese, all types of curries and the superb Steak & Ale Pie, using Tillerman's Tipple. The Sunday roast is pretty good value too at £5.95 – pork, beef or lamb accompanied by eight fresh vegetables.

To get full value from all this wonderful food and drink, you need to arrive by boat or by train. Alvechurch Station, with connections from Redditch and Birmingham, is only two minutes walk away. Enjoy the serenity of the canal and the pub's sensual pleasures.

Robin Smitheet

On the Grand Union Canal at Stoke Bruerne. There is always plenty of activity around the lock and the canal museum, seen here in the background. Across the canal from the musem is The Boat Inn.

GRAND UNION CANAL (MAIN LINE)

Limehouse Basin (London) to Salford Junction (Birmingham)
158 miles/178 locks/5 tunnels

The Godfather of British canals; as its name suggests, this waterway is on a truly grand scale, featuring broad locks and impressive engineering structures. The Grand Union system resulted from an amalgamation of existing canals in 1929 to provide a route linking London with the Derbyshire/Nottinghamshire coalfields and with Birmingham.

London's waterways are all things to all men: splendidly elegant at Little Venice; fairly dire at Hackney and Islington; bustling and lively at Camden Lock; anonymously suburban at Uxbridge.

The finest section of the Grand Union Canal is where it ascends the Chilterns, reaching its summit at Tring. Two branches – the Wendover Arm and the Aylesbury Arm – punctuate the canal's northward passage.

The canal enhances the environs of Milton Keynes; open spaces and wooded areas border the waterway to pleasing effect. Some 20 miles further north, Stoke Bruerne is a picture-postcard canal village, set in fine countryside and richly endowed with thatched stone cottages; a couple of inns and a museum complete the scene. Beyond Blisworth Tunnel (3,065 yards long) the Northampton Arm leads to the River Nene, whilst the GU drives relentlessly onwards to Norton Junction, where the Leicester Section heads off to the right.

Braunston is another famous canal village to enliven the journey north before Leamington Spa and Warwick provide ample opportunity to spend a little cash. At Hatton, a mightily impressive flight of 21 locks elevates the canal 146ft 6in out of the Avon Valley.

From Kingswood Junction a short arm leads to the Stratford upon Avon Canal, but the GU itself approaches Birmingham. At Camp Hill, the locks are narrow as the canal descends to join the Birmingham & Fazeley's Digbeth Branch for access to the city centre.

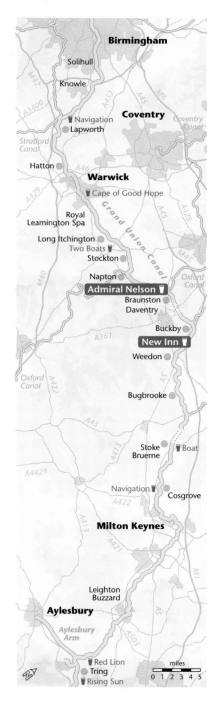

THE ADMIRAL NELSON

Braunston, Daventry, Northamptonshire

PUB FACTS

Location	Braunston, Daventry, Northamptonshire NN11 7HJ
Tel	01788 890075
Email	mail@admiralnelson-braunston. fsnet.co.uk
Proprietors	Diane Scott and Endaf Jones
Opening hours	Vary between summer and winter. Open all day in summer months, please call for details.
Food served	During opening hours, as above. Traditional food with the emphasis on quality, with the addition of dishes like Mussels and Wild Rabbit Pie for the more adventurous. Booking recommended.
Real ales	Most recently, Black Sheep Best Bitter, Black Sheep Ale and Timothy Taylor's Landlord
Moorings	Above Top Lock and below Nelson Lock

I first discovered the canals in 1965 when my wife, Sarah, and I hired a boat from Concoform Marine at Weedon. It was a cabin cruiser; there were very few modern narrowboats on the waterways at that date. And, despite the stern strictures of the boatyard, we ventured into the 'uncharted waters' of the BCN – murky oil-stained canals, snaking past factories belching out fire and smoke. The old British Waterway maps ended as you entered Brummagem and we were on our own. Literally. We didn't see another boat until we were on the Coventry Canal.

Once back on the Grand Union, we stopped off at the Admiral Nelson, beautifully situated alongside lock three (Nelson Lock) of the Braunston flight. It was a small pub in those days. We drank a pint of Watneys Red Barrel and gazed at the shrivelled ham sandwiches under a plastic cover and we were not tempted.

How things have changed. The Nelson has expanded, the food is delicious and the beer is real. But it manages to retain the atmosphere of a genuine canalside pub. You can still play Northamptonshire skittles with its lethal 'cheeses' and meet some of the ex-working boatmen who live in Braunston and, if you're lucky, have your glass shaken by the resident ghost.

The building was a farmhouse before it became a pub. Braunston was a thriving farming community and remained peaceful and unchanged until the arrival of the Oxford Canal in 1774, followed by the Grand Union or Grand Junction Canal, as it was then, in 1800. The farmhouse was conveniently situated to be converted into a pub, to service first the navvies building the canal and then the boat people working their way up or down the six locks. There were three more pubs between the Nelson and the top lock. As we all know, it's thirsty work being on a canal.

It always has been so: John Hollingshead was travelling as a passenger in a flyboat in 1858 and recounted his experiences in *Household Words*. They reached a 'long low-roofed tavern' just outside Braunston: "We left the barge in a body to try the strength and flavour of the tavern's best ale…

Through a door at the end was seen the grocery department, communicating with and terminating in, the butcher's shop. The passage formed such a tempting vista of food that we could not delay a moment, and, leaving the boatmen to drink their ale, we rushed through and immediately purchased several pounds of beefsteak." This tavern could well have been the Admiral Nelson, which was also, reputedly, visited by Charles Dickens on a canal trip. The pub was being run by a nephew, who sold him a Buckby can.

So, sit outside the pub on the lockside or below the hump-backed bridge on the canalside and enjoy a pint in the sunshine. But don't worry if it's raining, pop inside and have a paella in the parlour and imagine when cows were milked in the restaurant and killed in the games room (it was the abattoir).

The Admiral Nelson will never again have Charles Dickens popping in for a pint, or Leslie Morton of the Willow Wren Company using it as his office and regaling his boaters with tales. Nor will you see a dubious pork pie or a limp ham batch. But you might grab an anecdote from one of Braunston's many ex-boat people or, if you're really lucky, watch the Mikron Theatre Company performing outside as the sun sets!

THE NEW INN

Buckby Wharf, Northamptonshire

PUB FACTS

Location	Buckby Wharf, Northamptonshire NN6 7PW
Tel	01327 844747
Proprietors / landlords	Jo & George Summerskill
Opening hours	Mon–Sat 12pm–11pm, Sunday 12pm–10.30pm
Food served	12pm–2.30pm, 6pm–9pm
Real ales	Green King IPA, Frog Island beers of Northampton
Moorings	Above and below the top lock of the Buckby flight

On my very first day of boating, six locks were quite enough for the first afternoon. So, we tied up just above the last lock and decided to sample the delights of the New Inn, handily situated on the lockside. It was a lovely little pub and what delighted us was that a pint of bitter was 1/9d (9p). We were from London where 2/3d a pint was cheap. With such economies, we were forced to stay all evening and made our first acquaintance with working boat people and with Henry Grantham, the lockkeeper on the Buckby flight.

The New Inn today has several rooms all running off a central bar area, real fires, a skittles table, a pianola with rolls of 1920s music and, of course, a ghost. The pub opened as a coaching inn in the 1800s. Dick Turpin allegedly stayed there while riding up Watling Street (now the very busy A5). But, as he died in 1736, this is probably as likely as Good Queen Bess having slept there.

What is definitely known is that John Lowe was the landlord in 1869 and, in 1898, Elizabeth Thompson also ran a shop there. Until 1910, there was the Anchor Brewery at the wharf and five other pubs as well.

It was around then that the landlord, Jimmy Lovelock, decided to make water cans (Buckby cans, as they have become known generically) for the passing boat people. His daughter, Matilda, decorated them beautifully with the now familiar roses and castles. But her fate was sealed when she fell in love with one of the boatmen. Dad was distinctly displeased when she asked if she could go travelling with him and refused her request. In despair, she hanged herself… and now she sits at Table 11. Customers and staff are 'aware' of her presence: glasses are whipped off the table and, on one occasion, a pint of Stella fell off the table and landed on the floor – and not a drop was spilt.

During the Second World War, the trainees, the all-women boat crews recruited off the land, used to call at the New Inn, as Margaret Cornish recalls in her book, *Troubled Waters*: "… had drinks at the New Inn, where we had bought some of Lord Woolton's infamous pies".

You can still buy locally-painted Buckby cans at the pub and now you can sample an array of home-cooked food, including Steak and Guinness pie. You can sit out on the terrace and watch the boats lock through, or you can venture inside, play skittles, try the pianola and, of course, sit at Table 11. If your glass is mysteriously taken away, just say: "It's only Matilda". Or move quickly to another table.

OTHER PUBS WORTH TRYING

Grand Union Canal

NAVIGATION

Lapworth

Old Warwick Road, Lapworth, Solihull, West Midlands B94 6NA

Tel: 01564 783337

Lapworth, where the Grand Union and Stratford canals 'kiss' before parting again, is a canal settlement of great interest, and the Navigation more than does it justice. On the Grand Union, it combines a traditional bustling locals' bar with real fire, with a more relaxed dining room to the rear. The food is delicious (and very, very plentiful), and the beer and cider great. A welcome real inn in an area over-burdened with pricey gastropubs.

CAPE OF GOOD HOPE

Warwick

66 Lower Cape, Warwick CV34 5DP

Tel: 01926 498138

www.capeofgoodhope.co.uk

Undoubtedly the best pub for a good few miles, and with one of the best locations on the canals, too, just above the Cape Flight. Well kept and varied ales. If you're really hungry, try the 'Cape Fear' grill – but be sure to unballast your boat first.

TWO BOATS INN

Long Itchington, Warwickshire

Southam Road, Long Itchington,
Warwickshire CV47 9QZ
Tel: 01926 812640
www.2boats.co.uk

Long Itchington is surprisingly well supplied with pubs and for our money this is the best of the bunch. A friendly red brick pub with excellent ale and towpath tables. It's popular with boaters – there are moorings outside – and cyclists on the Sustrans Bristol–Rugby route which passes here.

THE BOAT INN

Stoke Bruerne,
Northamptonshire

Stoke Bruerne,
Northamptonshire NN12 7SB
Tel: 01604 862428
www.boatinn.co.uk

A famous pub in the quintessential canal village, working boatmen have refilled here since the 19th century – indeed, the same family has owned it for 125 years. The modern restaurant is a nod to the leisure age, but doesn't detract from the atmosphere.

NAVIGATION

Cosgrove, Milton Keynes

Thrupp Wharf, Cosgrove,
Milton Keynes MK19 7BE
Tel: 01908 543156
www.navigationinn.net

Just ten minutes drive from central Milton Keynes (that's by car not boat), a traditional pub with pleasant canalside garden. Popular both summer (check out the sunsets) and winter (roaring log fires). There's a good selection of real ales, a varied menu, and entertainment (bands, solo artists etc) is provided on Friday evenings.

RED LION

Marsworth, Buckinghamshire

Vicarage Road, Marsworth, Tring,
Hertfordshire HP23 4LU
Tel: 01296 668366

Located near Bridge 130, this is both a village local and popular boaters' pub. There is a well kept garden, bars on two levels and a good choice of real ales. (The cider is good too.) Food is served both lunchtimes and evenings and winter boaters will relish the open fire after a day out in the cold.

RISING SUN

Berkhamsted, Hertfordshire

George Street, Berkhamsted,
Hertfordshire HP4 2E
Tel: 01442 864913

This select Home Counties town is awash with convivial pubs but this a boaters' favourite thanks to its authentic unspoilt character and good range of real ales. There's a small canalside garden and meals are served lunchtimes and evenings.

KENNET & AVON NAVIGATION

Reading to Bristol
93 miles/104 locks/2 tunnels

It's impossible to overstate the appeal of this wonderful coast-to-coast waterway. Reopened in full in 1990, the K&A passes through some of the finest scenery – and elegant market towns – that central southern England has to offer.

Bustling Reading – at the River Kennet's confluence with the Thames – gives little indication of the delights to come further west. Soon, however, the K&A establishes itself as a rural waterway par excellence. Part canal, part river, it traverses a low-lying landscape of water meadows and marshland. Features of interest come along thick and fast: Garston Lock, one of the few remaining turf-sided locks on the waterway, Aldermaston Wharf with its visitor centre, and a host of swing bridges to exercise boat crews.

Newbury is a thoroughly welcoming town, full of fine shops, restaurants and wine bars situated conveniently close to the canal. Hungerford – though smaller – is equally attractive. But however much you may have enjoyed the journey thus far, the best of the K&A is just beginning as you cross the county border into Wiltshire. Little and Great Bedwyn are delightful canalside villages set amidst the gentle hills of East Wiltshire. Then comes Crofton Pumphouse, open to the public daily in season – steam

weekends are held from time to time. Perhaps the finest section of all lies between Pewsey and Devizes, as the canal traces a delightful course through the Vale of Pewsey, overlooked by the chalky Marlborough Downs.

The famous Devizes lock flight lowers the canal 237 feet into the Avon Valley – a fabulous feat of engineering set amidst fabulous countryside. Bradford-on-Avon is followed by two fine aqueducts: Avoncliff and Dundas. And so to Bath – quite simply the most beautiful city in the UK. Any visitor to this Georgian treasure trove is lucky, those who arrive by canal boat are luckiest of all. Enjoy the Roman Baths, the Abbey, Pulteney Bridge, Georgian crescents, tea shops and fine restaurants, etc, etc.

Thereafter, several miles of pleasurable cruising on the River Avon are on the agenda before your arrival in the ancient seaport of Bristol. There's much to enjoy here, including the mighty *SS Great Britain*, located in the Floating Harbour. Don't miss the Clifton Suspension Bridge, with its informative visitor centre, or the city's zoo, nearby.

THE BARGE INN

Pewsey, Wiltshire

PUB FACTS

Location	Honey Street, Pewsey, Wiltshire SN9 5PS
Tel	01672 851705
Email	adrian@the-barge-inn.com
Lessees	Adrian & June Potts
Opening hours	Mon–Wed 11.30am–11.30pm, Thu–Sat 11.30am–12.30am, Sun 11.30am–12am
Food served	12pm–2.30pm, 7pm – 9pm
Real ales	Black Sheep Best Bitter, Deuchars IPA, Wychwood's Hobgoblin
Moorings	Outside pub
	Good campsite facilities behind pub for tents and caravans

Thank goodness the Kennet & Avon was re-opened for through navigation in 1990. It's an exceptionally beautiful waterway, a mixture of the rivers Kennet and Avon and canal. It has many highlights, not least the Vale of Pewsey, overlooked by the Marlborough Downs. Looking down on you, as you dawdle along admiring the scenery, is the White Horse of Alton Barnes, cut in 1812. Pull in outside the Barge Inn at Honey Street. You'll be able to take a longer look at the White Horse and the staggering skyline, whilst savouring the delights of this fascinating place.

Honey Street Wharf was owned by Robbins, Lane & Pinniger until the late 1940s. They built wooden boats for the canal and operated their own barge, *Unity*, carrying softwood from Avonmouth. The

welcoming place it is today. Used by boaters, campers, walkers, locals and visitors alike, it offers well-kept beers, fresh home-cooked seasonal food and a friendly atmosphere. Dogs wander in, people have heated discussions (they even have a Monday Club where folk meet to have a good natter) and impromptu music sessions just happen (they also organise music festivals). In the winter, you snuggle round the lovely wood burning stove, roasting chestnuts. *The Wench is Dead*, with Inspector Morse, was filmed here.

But the large mural covering the pool room ceiling gives away the most remarkable aspect of this pub. It is the unofficial headquarters for followers of the crop circle phenomenon, and people come from all over the world to make their own minds up about the veracity of this cult.

Barge Inn, alongside, was built in 1810 to coincide with the opening of the canal. As well as being a brew and ale house, other services included an abattoir and butchers, bakery, smoke shed, coach house, stables and cart shed.

The original building burnt down in 1858. The fire brigade took eight hours to come from Devizes and, after the fire was finally extinguished, according to the Devizes and Wiltshire Gazette, "the cellars were entered and there was nothing but drunkenness and confusion."

There's much talk of ley and energy lines and, even, little green aliens. Is it all one big hoax? Certainly the current crop circle makers create beautiful works of art (there are many photos in the pub) but occasionally one of them will say, "I didn't make that" and then another will say, "Well, I didn't make it". Maybe the farmers are cashing in themselves? Who knows.

A plaque at the gable end of the pub commemorates the rebuilding in six months. It still looks the same to this day apart from, for safety reasons, smaller chimney stacks and the imposing lookout tower (for spotting arriving barges?), which rotted away many years ago.

The Potts became landlords in 1993. The building was plagued by rats, flies and bees, and the garden was completely overgrown but, undeterred, June and Adrian proceeded to turn the pub into the wonderfully

BARGE INN

Seend Cleeve, near Melksham, Wiltshire

PUB FACTS

Location	Seend Cleeve, near Melksham, Wiltshire SN12 6QB
Tel	01380 828230
Email	bargeinn@wadworth.co.uk
Proprietors	Wadworth & Co Ltd
Licensee	Sarah & Paul Haynes
Opening hours	11am–11pm
Food served	12pm–3pm, Snacks 3pm–5pm, 6pm–10pm, Lite Bites £4.50–£7.20, Starters £3.95–£6.50, Mains £7.95–£12.95
Real ales	Wadworth beers
Moorings	Outside pub or on towpath side opposite

If you have spent most of the day descending the Caen Hill flight, an energetic and exciting experience, keep going for a short while past beautiful countryside and through a couple of swing bridges and you'll arrive at the first of the Seend Cleeve flight of five. What more locks? Don't despair. Go through four of them and you'll arrive at your haven for the night – the Barge Inn. There you will find sufficient sustenance to ease your aching limbs.

The building's been around since 1805. It was originally a wharf house, bakery and stables, servicing the canal and was owned by the Duke of Somerset's family. There's very little sign of it today but this was a busy industrial area in the nineteenth century. When the railway arrived in the 1850s, Seend Ironworks was opened to exploit the iron ore waiting to be mined.

Loads of iron ore were taken by rail to the canal and thence to Bristol and on to Wales for smelting. Despite the abandonment of the ironworks in 1876, iron ore continued to be quarried until 1946. There are some reminders of this by-gone age – the nearby terrace houses were lived in by the ironworkers, whilst the manager's house was of much larger and elegant proportions and still sits atop a hill above the canal.

Eventually, the wharf building became the Barge Inn and resident there in 1916 was the 'Wiltshire Giant', Fred Kempster, who stood a modest 8 feet 2 inches.

When Mikron visited the pub in 1994, the building remained unchanged. I remember the landlady, Dilys Williams, who was trying to keep this simple pub going after her husband's death. Jim is remembered as a great character whose main role in life was supplying not just the locals' need for ale but anything they required really. A shovel, a fork, a generator – he'd have it for you the next day.

Since then the pub has been extended front and back and now has a large restaurant, where you can build up your muscle power for lockwheeling with, for example, pan fried crevettes, followed by locally sourced lamb rump. All the food is freshly made by the landlord, Paul, and his two assistants.

There's an attractive canalside garden adorned with an old cart, and barrels and flowers and cartwheels dotted about the place. It's a restful place to watch the sometimes unrestful activity of boats tying up on the opposite bank to water up.

Many boaters do frequent the pub but it's also a destination venue for car drivers. Locals tend only to use the pub in winter but you still get characters. While I was there, a large man arrived on his heavily laden bicycle. He was travelling from Bath to Stratford along the canal towpaths and his exhausting regimen was "a pint every thirty miles". He downed his first pint of the day, soaked his handkerchief in the canal, stuck it on his head against the intense morning heat and proceeded on his way: "Reading tonight!"

While there, have a stroll into Seend Cleeve and Seend, villages connected with the woollen, iron and stone quarrying and iron ore industries of the past. Flemish clothiers settled here in the fifteenth and sixteenth centuries. In the 1700s, John Aubrey wrote, "They built several good houses, yet remaining. I know not any village so remote from London that can show the like."

OTHER PUBS WORTH TRYING

Kennet & Avon Navigation and the Bristol Avon

DUNDAS ARMS

Kintbury, Berkshire
53 Station Road, Kintbury,
Berkshire RG17 9UT
Tel: 01488 658263
www.dundasarms.co.uk

Something of a local institution, and in the same ownership for 30 years, this pub serves excellent real ale from small breweries, fine wines, and interesting bar snacks and full meals.

LOCK, STOCK AND BARREL

Newbury, Berkshire
Northbrook Street, Newbury,
Berkshire RG14 1AA
Tel: 01635 580550

A Fullers pub – so you can expect a decent pint of London Pride – in a great town centre location looking down on the canal. The LSB is now gaining a reputation for live music, too.

FRENCH HORN

Pewsey, Wiltshire
Marlborough Road, Pewsey,
Wiltshire SN9 5NT
Tel: 01672 562443

An attractive, traditional pub with a beer garden overlooking the canal. Above average food and local Wadworths ale.

THREE MAGPIES

Sells Green, Wiltshire
Sells Green, Seend, Melksham,
Wiltshire SN12 6RN
Tel: 01380 828389
www.three-magpies.co.uk

The magpies were three chattering sisters who owned the pub in the 19th century. The welcome is friendly; there's Wadworths beer and Westons cider; the service is famously efficient. Food is traditional pub grub, done well.

BARGE INN

Bradford-on-Avon, Wiltshire
17 Frome Road, Bradford-on-Avon,
Wiltshire BA15 2EA
Tel: 01225 863403

In Bradford-on-Avon the towpath teems with walkers and cyclists and the fastest way through is by boat – but do stop at the Barge for the real ale, which changes frequently, and the beer garden.

THE APPLE

Bristol
Welsh Back, Bristol BS1 4SB
Tel: 0117 925 3500
www.applecider.co.uk

A pub on a boat! The Apple, a barge in Bristol's famous Floating Harbour, has a range of real ciders and perrys, from gentle still ciders to skull-clenching scrumpys; the food is juicy. The clientele is young (except when we turn up) and lively.

LEE & STORT NAVIGATION
AND LONDON WATERWAYS

River Lee, Limehouse Basin to Hertford: 27 miles/19 locks
River Stort, Feilde's Lock to Bishop's Stortford: 14 miles/15 locks

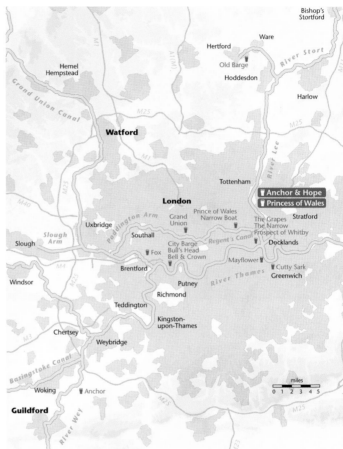

Any navigation which passes, as does the Lee, through the likes of Limehouse, Bow, Hackney, Tottenham and Enfield is not destined to win too many beauty competitions. But, and it's a huge but, this area is undergoing regeneration following London's successful bid for the 2012 Olympics. In any case, the Lee does substantially improve in the vicinity of Waltham Abbey, which has twice staged the Inland Waterways Association's National Festival & Boat Show in recent years. Water meadows and willow trees accompany the river through Broxbourne – arguably the most attractive section – before the head of navigation is reached at Hertford.

The River Stort is perhaps a more attractive river, traversing as it does some enjoyable countryside on the Essex/Hertfordshire border. Sawbridgeworth – still a pleasant market town despite expansion in recent years – enhances the appeal of this comparatively little known river. Navigation ends at Bishop's Stortford, another bustling town with good shops, pubs and restaurants.

Rural splendour at Stansted Abbots on the River Lee.

PRINCESS OF WALES

Clapton, London E5

PUB FACTS

Location	146 Lea Bridge Road, London E5 9QB
Tel	020 8533 3463
Email	powclapton@hotmail.com
Lessee	Tony Barratt
Opening hours	12pm–12pm, Sun 12pm–10.30pm
Food served	12pm–3pm, 6pm–9pm, Sun 12pm–5pm
Real ales	Young's Bitter and Special, Wells' Bombardier and seasonal ales
Moorings	Outside the pub

The River Lee is a tributary of the Thames and, when it gets to its tidal mouth, Bow Creek, it has travelled from Hertford, 27½ miles further north. It has been navigable from the 13th century but it was in the late 18th century that improvements were made that turned it into a very busy commercial waterway. Today, there is very little sign of that.

The Prince of Wales is a great pub - or rather the Princess of Wales. In 1997, shortly after the death of Diana, John Young, the chairman of Young's Brewery in Wandsworth, who owned the pub, requested that the name be changed in memory of the Princess. Many of the locals still call it the Prince or POW and, inside, the many photos of Diana adorning the walls are alongside those of the current and previous Princes of Wales.

It's a fine building dating from the 1860s. The large, comfortable lounge is wood panelled and lit by vintage lamps. There is a separate, no-nonsense public bar. The early censuses reveal that Caleb and Amelia Day and their family were landlords there from 1861 until at least 1891. Young's took over the pub in 1964 and it is now owned by the Wells Young Company.

It's a very welcoming oasis for boaters travelling out of London to explore the upper reaches of the Lee and the winding delights of the River Stort, and for walkers and cyclists who are in need of good refreshment. The beers are excellent and go well with the appetising pub grub on offer. In summer, you can drink the honey-laced Waggle Dance with your smoked haddock and spinach fishcakes. Or why not try a Double Chocolate Stout with your chocolate fudge cake?

The POW is a pub that caters for everyone, with darts teams playing on a Tuesday and Thursday, a quiz night on a Wednesday and live bands (often jazz) on a Saturday evening. And you will almost certainly meet Jack. He's a Jack Russell who is devoted both to the pub and the customers. When the previous landlord moved to Blackpool, Jack couldn't settle to his new life by the seaside and was returned to the Princess of Wales. Jack was back.

There's plenty of outdoor space for summer eating and drinking and, in 2012, there will need to be. The Olympic Park is being constructed just downstream on Hackney Marshes. The character of the area will be radically changed and will no doubt bring many benefits to the River Lee and the Bow Backwaters and to the Princess of Wales. Not all the locals are in favour, however, fearing that, after all the razzmatazz of the Games is over, the area and the people living there will again be forgotten.

Whatever is in store, get along to the POW now and enjoy the pleasures of a real London pub.

ANCHOR & HOPE

Clapton, London E5

PUB FACTS

Location	15 High Hill Ferry, London E5 9HG
Tel	020 8806 1730
Email	matthew@withey1.fsnet.co.uk
Licensee	Matthew Withey
Opening hours	Summer (Easter–October): 12pm–11pm, Winter: Mon–Fri 1pm–11pm, Fri–Sun 12pm–11pm
Food served	Filled rolls always available except Sun, when there are nibbles on the bar
Real ales	Fuller's London Pride and ESB, plus changing guest beers, eg Castle Rock's Harvest Pale, Fuller's Discovery, Wychwood's Hobgoblin
Moorings	Outside pub

The Anchor & Hope is a gem. It's one of the smallest pubs in England, perched on a corner site overlooking the River Lee and with cottages and houses around it. It was built over 150 years ago and used to be owned by the Tolly Cobbold Brewery until taken over by Fuller's. Some of the locals still refer to it as the Tolly. It was one of three pubs very close to each other alongside the river. The Beehive closed fifty years ago, the Robin Hood more recently in order for more housing to be erected.

Up until his death, the pub had been run for 52 years by Les. He never took a holiday and was proud of his OBE. His portrait is over the fireplace and from there he continues to keep an eye on the clientele.

Now, Matthew and his wife, Shirley, run the pub. They are very young but are aware of the unchanging nature of the Anchor & Hope. Matthew's parents still live close by on the riverside and he remembers, as a school kid, not being able to get into his house – there were so many people thronging outside the pub.

And that's the thing. Get twenty people inside and it's packed out. Mind you, they still have room for a darts board tucked around the only corner of the bar.

So, whatever the weather, but particularly in the summer, the punters spread along the riverfront. They are a most eclectic bunch. For a start, the core of diehard regulars is a melting pot of nationalities from all parts of the globe. And the visitors can be anybody from passing boaters, walkers and cyclists, guitar-playing hippies with dogs on strings to a complete family with little baby and granny. There's a man who often turns up for a pint in his Jaguar.

They're all here for the beer, of course, which is excellent. Apart from the delicious beers from Fuller's (do try, but be wary of, the ESB at 5.5%), Matthew says he gets through two guest ales a week. But it's much more than that. It's the conviviality and the

atmosphere. The rumble of the trains passing over the nearby railway bridge is the only noise apart from the chatter of folk. There is a semi-rural feel about the place. A boat will chug by, a cormorant will fly past and, on the opposite bank, you have Walthamstow Marsh, which is one of the last surviving examples of natural marshland in the London area.

Everything about this place is a surprise. Get along there and sample it for yourself. Don't ask for the menu or the wine list and, as you stand hugger-mugger in the bar with a pint in your hand, be prepared to talk to anyone about anything.

OTHER PUBS WORTH TRYING

River Lee and London waterways

Limehouse area

How can one do justice to London's pubs in such a short space? Here's a whistlestop tour.

Start in Limehouse, where Gordon Ramsay has taken over the fabulously situated **Narrow** (Narrow Street, E14: 020 7592 7950) – it overlooks the entrance to Limehouse Basin, where the Regent's Canal meets the tidal Thames. Despite the celebrity chef, there's no compulsion to eat here (the food is, of course, mouthwatering): it's a great place to enjoy a pint.

For a different experience, pop down the road to the **Grapes** (020 7987 4396), a tiny, ancient-looking pub with river views and a good seafood restaurant upstairs. Also nearby is the **Prospect of Whitby** (Wapping Wall, E1: 020 7481 1095). Almost 500 years old and once a haunt of smugglers.

Greenwich area

Across the river, we like the down-to-earth, slightly grubby **Cutty Sark** – what else? – in Greenwich. Some 300 years old, its bowed front lends a nautical feel augmented by the fine riverside terrace. Good beer and filling food. (Ballast Quay, SE10: 020 8858 3146). A little further west, the **Mayflower** is the site where the eponymous boat set off on its way to Plymouth to pick up the Pilgrim Fathers, and on to the New World: it's a very pleasant pub today with good river views. (Rotherhithe Street, SE16: 020 7237 4088.)

Central London canals

London's canals are not blessed with as many pubs as the Thames, but there are still some fine ones to be found. The split-level **Narrow Boat** in Islington blurs the line between pub and bar, but still serves real ale and well-prepared, if pricey, food (St

Peter's Street, N1: 020 7288 9821). More pubby is the **Prince of Wales**, a stone's throw to the west, a traditional two-bar boozer popular with local CAMRA types (Sudeley Street, N1: 020 7837 6173). Out in Westbourne Park, we also like the **Grand Union**, a modern refit of a Victorian pub with top-quality pies and a canalside terrace (Woodfield Road, W9: 020 7286 1886).

Strand-on-the-Green

Well-heeled West London makes the most of its river, and the best concentration of pubs is at Strand-on-the-Green (W4), near Kew. The **Bell & Crown** is a Fullers establishment with a lovely conservatory and patio that just manages to resist the lurch into restaurantdom (020 8994 4164); the **Bull's Head** is a bit more foody, but still offers plenty of real ale (020 8994 1204); and the **City Barge** is a friendly, Tardis-like pub with a sought-after riverside terrace (020 8994 2148). Pop your head around all three doors and see which appeals.

Further afield

Finally, three destinations for the Londoner looking for a Saturday afternoon relaxing by the water. The **Old Barge**, on the River Lee in Hertford, has a superb selection of ale and cider, and a warm, cosy interior. There's jazz every other Thursday (Folly Island: 01992 581871). The **Fox**, in Hanwell, is a smashing 'real pub' with an annual beer festival, reasonably priced food and pleasant walking along the Grand Union's Hanwell Locks (Green Lane, W7: 020 8567 4021). And to the south, the **Anchor** at Pyrford Lock, on the River Wey near Woking, has a lovely situation on this quiet river and better-than-average beer (near Wisley: 01932 342507).

OXFORD CANAL

Oxford to Hawkesbury Junction (Coventry)
77 miles/43 locks/1 tunnel

From magical Oxford – city of bells – to more mundane Coventry, the Oxford Canal threads a delightful course through the South Midlands and has justifiably established itself as one of the most popular canals in the country.

Access from the Thames is via the Sheepwash Channel or, further upstream, the Dukes Cut. Thereafter the lovely River Cherwell accompanies you north (it actually forms the navigation for a short section) through a succession of picturesque villages, notably Thrupp, Shipton-on-Cherwell and the two Heyfords, Lower and Upper.

The rural idyll is shattered somewhat by the M40, which runs close to the canal for several miles; and then by Banbury, although the latter's waterfront has been extensively redeveloped in recent years with not entirely unpleasing results.

But then you arrive at Cropredy and all else is forgiven. Is there a finer village anywhere on the system? Not according to many well-travelled boaters. Moor by the lock, spend a summer's evening here and you will fall utterly under Cropredy's spell. The village is closely associated with the famous folk/rock group Fairport Convention, who have been regular performers at the annual music festival staged each August.

The remainder of the southern section of the Oxford is no anti-climax either, as it weaves its tortuous course through remote Warwickshire farmlands, all the way to Napton, complete with its famous hilltop windmill.

The northern section of the Oxford Canal was straightened in the 1830s and evidence remains of many of the old arms, some of them still spanned by elegant cast iron bridges. This length lacks the unique charm of the southern section but the scenery remains pleasant and predominantly rural all the way to Hawkesbury Junction and the link with the Coventry Canal.

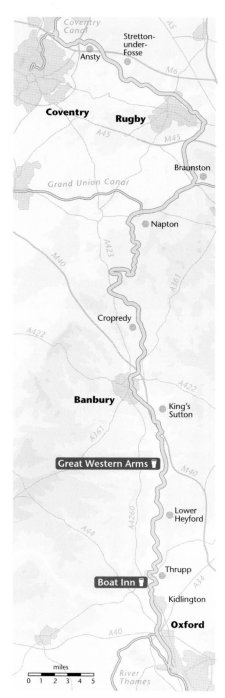

THE BOAT INN

Thrupp, Kidlington, Oxfordshire

PUB FACTS

Location	Canal Road, Thrupp, Kidlington, Oxfordshire OX5 1JV
Tel/Fax	01865 374279
Landlords	Jenny & Shane Bushel
Opening hours	Mon–Fri 11.30am–3pm, 5pm–11pm, Sat 12pm–11pm, Sun 12pm–10.30pm
Food served	Mon–Fri 12pm–2.15pm, 6pm–8.45pm (except Mon eves), Sat 12pm–3pm, 6pm–8.45pm, Sun 12pm–3pm
Real ales	Greene King IPA, Abbot and seasonal beers like Triumph and Suffolk Ale
Moorings	On the towpath between the pub and the lift bridge

Thrupp, or Tropp as it was called (meaning 'farm'), is now part of the very large village of Kidlington. It boasted three pubs at one time: the Three Horseshoes (now a private house), the Britannia (now the Jolly Boatman, canalside but also flanking the very busy A4260) and the Axe.

The Axe opened in 1753 in what was originally a farmhouse built from Cotswold stone with a slate roof. It changed its name to the Boat in 1790. It is no coincidence that this was the year the Oxford Canal was opened as far as Oxford itself.

So, the pub began its connection with the canal. It boasted a shop to service not only the hamlet but the passing horse drawn boats. Not a bad idea – a little shop as part of the pub. Canalside facilities are very scarce on this stretch of waterway. In fact, some boat people moved into the canalside cottages. No 6 was the home of the Coles family. Joseph Coles was working on the boats when he met the love of his life, Harriet, in Nuneaton. They moved to Thrupp in about 1804 and raised ten children. One of the daughters, Rose, married into the Beauchamps, a boating family, and ran one of the last working boats on the Oxford. Her daughter still lives in Kidlington.

Today, the people living in these (now) very desirable and (now) very expensive cottages still enjoy the pleasures a 'proper' pub can offer. The boat people and locals enjoyed making their own music in the Boat and there would often be a singalong accompanied by a fiddle and a melodeon. Nothing much has changed there: there's live folk music on the second Sunday of every month; there's Aunt Sally to be played in the large back garden (though the small planes taking off and landing from nearby Oxford Airport can sometimes be disconcerting); and cribbage and quizzes in the bar. It's a pub for discussing your day's boat trip – well, for discussing anything and everything. There's no television and no jukebox. Lovely.

There are bare boards, old canal pictures and separate rooms for eating. Virtually everything is home cooked, all the vegetables are fresh and specials are chalked up each day. While you're sitting there, supping your pint or stirring the cucumber in your Pimms, you may be thinking: "I recognise this pub". Yes, it featured in an episode of *Morse*.

THE GREAT WESTERN ARMS

Aynho, Oxfordshire

PUB FACTS

Location	Aynho Wharf, Station Road, Aynho, Oxfordshire OX17 3BP
Tel	01869 338288
Landlord	Frank Baldwin
Opening hours	Mon–Fri 12pm–3pm, 6pm–11pm, Sat 12pm–3pm, 6.30pm–11pm, Sun 12pm–3pm
Food served	Mon–Fri 12pm–2pm, 6pm–9pm, Sat/Sun 12pm–2pm (Starters £4.95–£6.95, Mains £8.75–£14.95)
Real ales	Hook Norton Bitter plus guest beers like St.Austell's Tribute and Charles Wells Bombardier
Rooms	Four double luxury en suite rooms with digital TV
Moorings	On the towpath opposite Aynho Wharf

The South Oxford Canal has many charms, not least its fair share of good canalside pubs. The Great Western Arms doesn't sound like a canalside pub and, strictly speaking, it isn't. It adjoins Aynho Station, once part of Brunel's glorious Great Western Railway. Now the trains roar past and the station, long closed, is a private house. But the pub is also part of Aynho Wharf, a remarkably well-preserved part of the fabric of the original Oxford Canal with a boatyard and a brick warehouse, which today functions as a shop catering to the needs of boaters.

A pub has been servicing boaters (or rather boatmen and women) on this site since the eighteenth century. In 1849, it was called the Alfred's Head. This was the year that Sir Thomas Cartwright became aware that the pub was very badly run, and very badly run down, and decided to buy it from the Great Western Railway, who had bought it from the canal company. The Cartwright family were the squires of the village of Aynho, which is one mile from the wharf, from 1616 until the 1950s.

Sir Thomas decreed that the old pub at Aynho wharf should be pulled down and a spanking new one built to replace it. This opened somewhere between 1864 and 1869, and was named the Great Western Arms. It is one of Hook Norton Brewery's 47 pubs. Still a small independent brewery, which has been in the same family since 1849, it's only a few miles away from the Great Western and well worth a diversion. It has a fine Victorian tower, a 25hp steam engine providing the motive power and shire horses, Consul, Major and Nelson, making local deliveries. Its real ales are delicious (personally tested, of course).

The Great Western Arms has been beloved by boaters and locals alike for many, many years; a pub where you could have a quiet drink, eat a steak or play bar billiards. The pub has changed and now concentrates on providing top class food. But it is still a fantastic pub.

Many of the changes are for the better. The large bar area remains, but the old children's room is an attractive dining area. The outdoor eating area is delightful and the old stables are now colonised by swallows. And the food – well, the chef knows his

way round fish and game and most other fare for that matter. All of it is home cooked and every sauce individually made: swordfish steak, sea bass, pheasant, gigot of lamb. We had crevettes, pan-fried with garlic and chilli, and game pie. Oh, please just go and try it for yourself.

The important thing to note is that you are welcome whether you have been boating, walking, cycling or driving. You can just have a pint of Hooky and read the newspapers and magazines or, if you want some pasta or a salad, that's fine as well. And you can browse your way round the GWR memorabilia, including a ticket dating from the 1800s and a bell from the front of a steam engine.

I think Sir Thomas would enjoy himself at the Great Western Arms and would have no plans for pulling it down and starting again.

RIVER THAMES

Teddington to Lechlade
125 miles/44 locks

With all due respect to the Norfolk Broads, the Thames is unquestionably Britain's premier holiday waterway, where pleasure boating first became popular in the 18th century. The river flows seductively across southern England, through a rich and varied landscape populated by rich (some very, very rich) and varied people. Teddington marks the lower limit of the non tidal navigation. Travelling upstream you encounter all manner of craft, from large trip boats down to punts and dinghies. The scenery is never less than gorgeous, and the roll call of riverside towns makes impressive reading: Kingston, Hampton (with its palace, park and maze), Sunbury, Windsor and Maidenhead are just some of the ports of call on the lower reaches.

Selecting the most beautiful section of this delectable river is well nigh impossible. But, perhaps the length between Cliveden and Reading may just shade it. Here the waterside houses are at their grandest,

Marlow and Henley need little introduction and Sonning Bridge and village are exquisitely charming.

But the Thames continues to enthrall, through Pangbourne, Goring, Dorchester and Abingdon. Goring is especially enchanting – a riverside village of quiet beauty. It was the final home of Sir Arthur 'Bomber' Harris – chief of RAF Bomber command in World War II – until his death in April 1984.

And then there's Oxford. The world famous university city doesn't necessarily turn its best face to the Thames (you'll have to hire a punt and explore the Cherwell for that), but Osney Lock is a good place to moor for a few hours and explore all the sights at your leisure.

Above Oxford the character of the river changes, becoming quieter, narrower and altogether more intimate. Thirty-two lonely miles take you to Lechlade and the end of a river journey with no equal anywhere in the British Isles.

THE MAYBUSH

Witney, Oxfordshire

PUB FACTS

Location	Newbridge, Witney, Oxfordshire OX29 7QD
Tel	01865 300624
Email	landlord@maybushinn.co.uk
Website	www.maybushinn.co.uk
Lessees	Stephen & Elizabeth Parker
Opening hours	Mon–Sat 11am–11pm, Sun 12pm–10.30pm (Closed Sun eve in winter)
Food served	11am–9pm
Real ales	Morland Original and Abbot Ale
Moorings	Outside pub and adjoining the field upstream of the bridge

For those of you who have never boated on the Thames above Oxford, you are in for a treat. The river takes on a very different character: the locks are much shorter, have balance beams and are manually operated (there's a lock-keeper, but give him or her a hand), the bridges are lower, and the channel twists and turns upon itself in a delightful way through remote-feeling countryside. There are fewer boats and no riverside villages, until you arrive at the navigable limit – the charming market town of Lechlade.

At Newbridge, the bridge has been there since 1250. It was built by monks from the priory at Deerhurst. They used stone from Taynton quarries, which was probably transported by boat down the River Windrush. The mouth (rather a generous term for a little stream) is opposite the pub. It was called New Bridge because it was the next bridge to

be built after the first one at Radcot two years earlier. It was modified in the fifteenth century, only for part of it to be destroyed during the Civil War by the Parliamentarians in order to prevent the Royalists escaping to Oxford.

The pub was originally a tollhouse for the bridge. It's not certain when it became a pub, but the name Maybush comes from medieval times when a landlord would hang a fresh branch over the door to indicate that a new brew was available. It was extended over the years and, a few years ago, a restaurant was added. It has one large bar area and a long terraced riverside garden. If you're not in a narrowboat, you can moor right outside the pub. You narrowboaters need to go further upstream, where there is a very pleasant meadow to tie alongside.

This is a hostelry where you can chill out. There is no jukebox, no background music, no darts, quizzes, game machines or TV. Food, drink and conversation are the order of the day. Of an evening, you may catch a gathering of socialising teachers or a couple who are meeting through a dating agency. Don't earwig. Oh, okay, do if you want, but try and have an intelligent conversation of your own, while you down a pint of Abbot Ale and eat the freshly cooked food – pie of the day, say, and veg from the pub garden.

Newbridge consists of the Maybush, the Rose Revived (on the opposite bank), a farm and a mill. The pub, obviously, relies on car trade as well as the boats. There are also the people walking the Thames Path. The towpath changes sides at Newbridge.

The old bridge is remarkable. Little did its builders know that there would be heavy lorries trundling across it instead of packhorses and wandering monks. If you are visiting in a car, you have to press a button to operate the traffic lights in order to get out of the pub car park. Another good reason for arriving by boat.

OTHER PUBS WORTH TRYING
Upper and Middle Thames

TROUT INN

Lechlade, Gloucestershire
St. John's Bridge, Faringdon Road,
Lechlade, Gloucestershire GL7 3HA
Tel: 01367 252313
www.thetroutinn.com

The furthest upstream of the many Trouts and a pleasant half-hour's walk along the river from Lechlade's Halfpenny Bridge. A friendly front bar, leads to a selection of dining rooms where you can choose from an astonishingly large menu. Appropriately, fish is a speciality, and local produce is used – yet this is no pretentious gastropub, but a welcoming, relaxing place you'd be proud to call your local. (If you were the lock keeper.) Live music and good beer.

SWAN HOTEL

Radcot, Oxfordshire
Radcot-on-Thames, Bampton,
Oxfordshire OX18 2SX
Tel: 01367 810220
www.swanhotelradcot.co.uk

The Thames above Oxford is hardly lacking in good pubs, and we're tempted simply to recommend a long weekend walking the Thames Path, stopping off at every one. But if we do have to choose, the Swan at Radcot deserves a mention, not least because it has day-boats for hire – so you can combine boating and beer (in that order)! There's accommodation, too, if you're walking the Path.

TROUT

Tadpole Bridge, Faringdon, Oxfordshire
Buckland Marsh, Faringdon,
Oxfordshire SN7 8RF
Tel: 01367 870382
www.trout-inn.co.uk

This Trout is decidedly more upmarket. The utterly delightful food, though not cheap, is the star attraction here: gastro it may be, but rather than relying solely on confits and terrines, the Trout also boasts fabulous bread, a Thursday sausage club, and excellent beer. Accommodation is available.

WATERMAN'S ARMS

Oxford
South Street, Osney,
Oxford OX2 0BE
Tel: 01865 248832

A down-to-earth backstreet pub overlooking the Thames just between Osney Lock and Osney Bridge. It is famed for the best Sunday roast in Oxford and attracts a dedicated local following. The moorings outside are a great base for exploring the city: because Osney Bridge is low, they tend to be colonised by narrowboats rather than the cruisers of downriver.

THE PLOUGH

Long Wittenham, Oxfordshire

High Street, Long Wittenham,
Abingdon, Oxfordshire OX14 4QH
Tel: 01865 407738

A little more down to earth than some pubs in the area. There is a nice long garden leading down to the river, moorings for a couple of boats, good quality home cooked food and a good range of draught beers. Plus a 'village local' atmosphere.

BARLEY MOW

Clifton Hampden, Oxfordshire

Clifton Hampden Road, Long
Wittenham Abingdon, Oxfordshire
OX14 3EH
Tel: 01865 407847

Jerome K Jerome described this as "the quaintest, most-old world inn up the river". Praise indeed – and it remains a wonderful pub. The white thatched building was built 650 years ago, has an enormous fireplace, lots of cosy nooks and crannies, and a fabulous garden. Lots of draught beers are served and a couple of real ales. The food is superb. Moorings are on the opposite bank.

THE BOATHOUSE

Wallingford, Oxfordshire

High Street, Wallingford,
Oxfordshire OX10 0BJ
Tel: 01491 833188

A lovely location, right beside Wallingford's historic bridge. Its riverside terrace is lovely too, the perfect place to while away the hours on a summer's day. Inside there is a big screen TV, pool table and lots of gaming machines, so this is hardly a quiet 'local'. Nevertheless, there's a good range of beers and food is served for most of the day.

THE SWAN

Pangbourne, Berkshire

Shooters Hill, Pangbourne, Reading,
Berkshire RG8 7DU
Tel: 0118 984 4494
www.swanpangbourne.com

An idyllic setting – overlooking Whitchurch Lock and Weir. The ancient inn's oak beams and open fires are perfect for cold, frosty evenings; the beautiful riverside garden really hits the spot on warm sunny days. The wide selection of ales, and tasty meals and snacks – served throughout the day – are a source of year-round enjoyment.

THE COMPLEAT ANGLER

Marlow, Buckinghamshire

Marlow, Buckinghamshire SL7 1RG
Tel: 0844 879 9128
www.macdonaldhotels.co.uk/
compleatangler

Ok, it's a hotel, but its bars are open to the public. To visit the Middle Thames and not have a drink at the Compleat Angler would be a bit like going to Paris and not seeing the Eiffel Tower.

EXETER CANAL

5 miles/3 locks

The Exeter Canal is the oldest canal in Britain to have been built with locks. It was opened in 1566, and improved in 1701 and 1830. It runs from the estuary of the River Exe at Turf Lock to its terminal basin at Exeter, alongside the Exe. This short waterway passes through most attractive scenery, with the scent and sounds of the estuary ever present, and is popular with the sailing fraternity of South Devon.

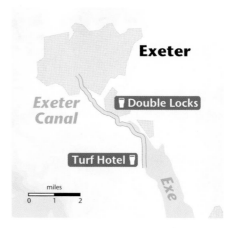

Double Locks looking towards Exeter.

DOUBLE LOCKS HOTEL

Exeter, Devon

PUB FACTS

Location	Canal Banks, Exeter, Devon EX2 6LT
Tel	01392 256947
Email	doublelocks@youngs.co.uk
Website	www.doublelocks.co.uk
	A Young's managed house
Opening hours	Summer: Mon–Sat 11am–12am, Sun 11am–10.30pm, October–Easter: Mon–Sat 11am–11pm, Sun 11am–10.30pm
Food served	Summer: Mon–Sat 12pm–9pm, Sun 12pm–8pm, October–Easter: Mon–Fri 12pm–2.30pm, 6pm–9pm, Sat 12pm–9pm, Sun 12pm–8pm
Real ales	Young's PA Bitter, Wells Bombardier, Otter Ale, O'Hanlon's Royal Oak
Moorings	Outside pub
	Camping available – phone ahead

You can get to the Double Locks Hotel by car, but it's not that easy. It's far better to make your way by bike or on foot. It's only one and a half miles from Exeter Canal Basin, which is well worth seeing anyway. But also how about travelling on the trip boat *Southern Comfort* or you can hire a canoe or book a rickshaw!

The Double Locks Hotel opened in 1827. There had been a lock house on the site since 1701 when the double lock was built. Although the canal was first completed in 1566, it proved inadequate for the size of vessels wanting to navigate to Exeter. It was widened, deepened and lengthened in 1698. The double lock accommodates two ships. It is 312 feet long and 26 feet wide.

When James Green, the West Country canal engineer, extended the canal to its full five miles length, he also converted the lock house into the hotel. He put in stables, a brewery and a cowshed.

It's an attractive brick built building nestling just below the lock. Wisteria drapes itself over the front door. Near here you will notice the remains of rail tracks running parallel to the lock. A horse-drawn truck used to carry smaller boats round the lock, which saved time and water.

Decking on several levels runs alongside the canal and behind is a large garden with tall fir trees. You enter the pub through a pleasant conservatory into an area where you order your food at a hatch. On the left is a proper bar with a tiled floor and a log fire. Have a look at the very interesting ceiling.

The food is all fresh and locally sourced. I had a delicious roasted vegetable and goat's cheese toasted ciabatta with fries, but you can have everything from chilli nachos to duck breast salad with hoi-sin dressing.

The pub has the canal on one side of it and the Riverside Valley Park on the other which runs from Cowley Bridge in Exeter to Topsham Ferry. There are extensive wetlands where you will be able to spot herons, kingfishers, shelducks, Brent geese and thousands of dragonflies.

When, and if, you tire of all this tranquillity, don't forget to visit the city of Exeter itself. When the Romans founded it in AD 50, they called it Isca Dumnoniorium, 'riverside settlement'. The riverside buildings, some of which are now cafes, bars and craft shops, are still well worth looking at, as is the magnificent 13th century cathedral.

TURF HOTEL

Exminster, Exeter, Devon

PUB FACTS

Location	Exminster, Exeter, Devon EX6 8EE
Tel	01392 833128
Email	info@turfpub.net
Website	www.turfpub.net
Lessees	Clive & Ginny Redfern
Opening hours	June–Aug: 11am–11pm, March–May: & Sept 11am–3pm, 6pm–11pm, Oct/Nov: weekends only 11.30am–6pm, Dec–Feb closed
Food served	April–Sept: Mon–Fri 12pm–2.30pm, 7pm–9pm, Sat 12pm–3pm, 7pm–9.30pm, Sun 12pm–3pm, March & Oct: weekends sometimes, only light snacks
Real ales	Otter Bitter & Otter Ale, O'Hanlon's Yellowhammer, Topsham & Exminster's Ferryman plus guest
Moorings	Outside pub on canal or on Exe estuary

This is bliss. A canalside pub that you cannot drive to. To get to this wonderful spot, you have to walk, cycle or boat. And where is this car-free haven? At the estuary end of the Exeter Ship Canal.

The Exeter Ship Canal owes its existence to the Countess of Devon, Isabella de Fortibus. In the sixteenth century, she had made the River Exe very difficult to navigate to Exeter by enlarging shoals and constructing fishing weirs. The reason? She wanted vessels to call instead at the port of Topsham which she owned.

Opened in 1556, it was the first canal to be built in Britain since the Romans constructed the Fossdyke & Witham, and was used by commercial shipping up to 400 tons as late as 1998. In 1827, the canal was extended further down the estuary to Turf. And this is where the splendid Turf Hotel was built, right alongside the lock, where accommodation was provided for the lockkeeper and for the crews of the sailing ships.

This is a remote pub. You can park your car and walk a mile down the towpath or along the sea wall from Powderham. You can cycle the five miles from Exeter. But the best option is to arrive by boat. There's a trip boat that comes down the canal in summer or take the wonderful journey from Topsham on board *Sea Dream*.

When you arrive, you are in another world. There's a vast garden with tall mature trees, where you can sit and admire the views right across the estuary to Exmouth. At low tide, the mud flats are the hunting grounds of many seabirds, including avocets and little egrets.

The pub itself is an attractive slate-hung, timber-framed building, and inside it is divided up into several rooms all leading one into the other. There are wooden floors, tables and chairs and bays with sash windows. There are maps on the walls of the River Exe and Devon, children's drawings and postcards and letters from

appreciative customers all over the world, and photos of the pub and some of the boats that have passed along the canal.

In the 1920s and '30s, the Turf Hotel was the place to go for whitebait teas in the upstairs room with views to the belvedere at Powderham. But gradually the place became neglected. It was threatened with closure and demolition but, thankfully, the Exeter Maritime Museum came to the rescue. They had the building listed and proceeded to restore it to its former glory. That renovation has been continued by Clive and Ginny Redfern who have been at the pub since 1990. The range of beers is tantalising – try the beautifully pale yellow Yellowhammer for a start. The food is yummy and good value. For lunch, try a brie, pesto and tomato toastie (£5) or spread your wings in the evening with a fillet of sea bass on a potato and chorizo cream (£12.95) washed down with a glass of wine from their good value list.

It's a place that makes you feel good to be alive, where one can appreciate the simple things of life. You'll be tempted to linger but don't miss the last ferry.

Trip boat Queen Boadicea *passes through the lift bridge beside the National Waterways Museum at Gloucester Docks. The museum charts the 200 year history of the docks and explores the trials and tribulations of canal life.*

GLOUCESTER & SHARPNESS CANAL
COTSWOLD CANALS

Gloucester to Sharpness: 16 miles/0 locks
Stroudwater Navigation, Framilode to Stroud: 8 miles
Thames & Severn Canal, Stroud to Lechlade: 33 miles

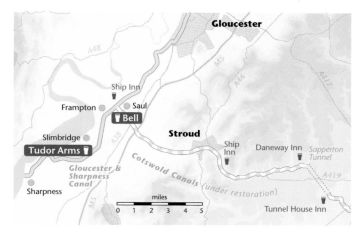

The Gloucester & Sharpness Canal could be accused of hiding its light under a bushel. Only a relatively few miles removed from the popular Avon Ring cruising circuit, the G&S attracts relatively few pleasure boaters to its charming waters – which is a shame, for a wealth of interest is packed into its short length.

Once Gloucester's fascinating docks and suburban outskirts have been left astern, the waterway traverses a gloriously remote landscape beside the broad waters of the River Severn, with far ranging views to the Forest of Dean. Numerous highlights vie for your attention: pretty Saul Junction; the immaculately kept swing bridges (all manned); the world renowned Slimbridge Wildfowl Centre, established by Sir Peter Scott on the marshes between the canal and the Severn; and divine Frampton-on-Severn, one of the most attractive villages in Gloucestershire. The canal concludes its journey to the Severn Estuary at Sharpness Docks, where moorings are provided for pleasure craft and you can, in the words of Otis Redding, "sit and watch the ships roll in". If you have the time you could even watch them roll away again.

Cotswold Canals

The Cotswold Canals comprise the Stroudwater Navigation and the Thames & Severn Canal. The former ran for some eight miles from the tidal Severn at Framilode to Wallbridge Basin on the outskirts of Stroud. Here it made an end-on junction with the Thames & Severn Canal, which continued for 33 miles on its spectacular journey through the Cotswold Hills to the River Thames at Lechlade. These canals are currently undergoing restoration with a target reopening date of 2018.

The Cotswold stone portal of Sapperton Tunnel on the Thames & Severn Canal.

BELL INN

Frampton-on-Severn, Gloucestershire

The Gloucester & Sharpness Canal took 36 years to construct. It was built as a ship canal and, unlike on the Continent, was one of the few navigations to be financed partly by the Government. Bypassing the River Severn, it ensured a much safer passage from Sharpness to Gloucester Docks and became very well used.

Sadly, today there is very little commercial traffic, but I still love this canal – the swing bridges, the classical style bridgemen's houses and the glimpses of the River Severn as it weaves and loops its way to the Bristol Channel growing bigger all the time. Just by Fretherne Bridge, there is a factory, which once belonged to Cadbury's. From 1916, chocolate crumb was taken by narrowboat to Bourneville, by the Severn & Canal Carrying Company and Cadbury's own fleet.

There are other reasons to stop here if you are boating, cycling, walking or on horseback. Just a short walk up the road is the village of Frampton-on-Severn, boasting, allegedly, the longest green in England. As you reach the green, the first place you see will be the Bell Inn.

Built in the 1700s, this creeper-clad

building has always been a pub. It has a bar area with a slate floor, a contemporary bistro with chunky wooden floor, tables and chairs and paintings of vegetables, and a more traditional style restaurant with blue and white tiles on the floor and relaxing paintings on the walls. (Good news – no mobile phones are allowed in the bistro or restaurant).

The Bell has a reputation for the beautiful condition of its cask ales. And it is also becoming very well known for the quality of its food. Try one of their snacks like a baguette filled with smoked salmon and crayfish. Or go for one of the day's specials: pan fried tiger prawns with garlic and parsley butter, followed by pork fillet stuffed with leek and bacon stuffing. Or why not push the boat out and, for £50 for two, treat yourself to Cypriot Fish Mezze featuring crayfish tails, smoked salmon, devilled whitebait, mussels, sardines, king prawns and a whole sea bass!

There's a pub farm as well. Go and see the Shetland ponies, the pygmy goats, Jacob sheep, rabbits, chickens and the boss, the cockerel.

Take your pint and sit and watch the cricket on the green right outside. This is quintessential England. The green is called Rosamund's Green after Jane Clifford, of the local family, who was born in the Bower at the Manor at Frampton in the 12th century. She was better known as 'Fair Rosamund'

PUB FACTS

Location	The Green, Frampton-on-Severn, Gloucestershire GL2 7EP
Tel	01452 740346
Fax	01452 740544
Email	hogben@gotdsl.co.uk
Website	www.bellatframpton.co.uk
Manager	Matthew Foxall
Opening hours	Mon–Sat 11am–12am, Sun 12pm–12am
Food served	12pm–9pm Prices from £3.50 to £17.50
Real ales	Changing guest beers including Abbot Ale & Sharp's Doom Bar
Moorings	On the towpath side near to Fretherne swingbridge, 10 minutes walk from pub
Rooms	4 rooms £60–£90 per room including Continental breakfast

and was the mistress of Henry II and rival to the jealous Queen Eleanor.

The Manor and the 18th century Frampton Court, with its staggeringly beautiful Orangery, are two of many fine buildings on the Green, plus duck ponds, horse chestnuts and a very useful post office and stores.

If you're not in a boat, you can stay the night at the Bell in one of their lovely suites overlooking the Green. If you've ridden here, the pub will even stable your horse for the night.

TUDOR ARMS

Slimbridge, Gloucestershire

PUB FACTS

Location	Shepherd's Patch, Slimbridge, Gloucestershire GL2 7BP
Tel	01453 890306
Email	ritatudorarms@aol.com
Proprietor	Rita Rock
Opening hours	Mon–Sat 11am–11pm, Sun 12pm–11pm
Food served	12pm–9pm
Real ales	Six real ales on at any one time
Moorings	On the towpath side of the canal near to Patch Bridge
Rooms	12 rooms in the adjacent Lodge from £45–£58 per night including breakfast

Slimbridge was originally Slime Bridge, an area of marshland alongside the River Severn. Gradually, during the 16th and 17th centuries, this land was reclaimed. Called the New Grounds, it became the home for pasturing cattle and sheep and an ideal spot for setting decoys and shooting ducks.

Even then, this area still had a tendency to flood when spring tides and bad weather coincided. The shepherds would move their sheep to higher ground – hence Shepherd's Patch.

Shepherd's Patch is a great place to tie up if you're boating or to visit by any other method of transport that takes your fancy. Just down the road towards the river is the Slimbridge Wildfowl & Wetlands Trust, founded by Peter Scott. This is an absolute must on anyone's itinerary. Another excellent reason for stopping at Shepherd's Patch is to visit the Tudor Arms. Just a few yards from the swing bridge, the building began life in the 1700s as a smallholding with a large orchard (where the car park is today), abundant with apple and pear trees. There was a cider press and much of this heady brew was sold to the local farmers.

When the navigators arrived to start building the Gloucester & Sharpness in the early nineteenth century, the house was licensed to sell both cider and beer. And that's how it stayed until the late 1950s when the pub gained a full on licence.

The Tudor Arms has grown since those days. The original bar no longer has a tin roof, and gone is the monstrous gas-burning fire where the cider was warmed up a little on chilly days. There are now lots of different spaces, including a light and pleasant conservatory and a new heated patio with large parasols and glass windows round the side.

But you can still eat and drink in the barn. Admittedly, the animals have gone and there is no hay in the loft anymore, although you can sit up there with the old wheel and handle of the hoist which brought the bales up to the loft.

The barn is now known as the Rorty Crankle restaurant (my research reveals this to mean 'enjoyable angular prominence'!). You can eat here or anywhere you choose in the pub. The food is made on the premises and the menu changes daily. Try grilled Barnsley chop (£8.95), oxtail in a red wine sauce (£8.25) or snack on baguettes, ploughman's or jacket potatoes. Most of the beers are from small local breweries and excellent, but don't forget to try Mole's Black Rat cider.

All in all, a great pub with much history and something to offer everyone. Peter Scott used to visit the Tudor Arms when he stayed in the building opposite, which was the Patch Hotel. In those days he hadn't come to Slimbridge to watch birds but to kill them. He was a wildfowler!

OTHER PUBS WORTH TRYING

Gloucester & Sharpness Canal and the Cotswold Canals

SHIP INN

Upper Framilode, Gloucestershire

Upper Framilode, Gloucestershire
GL2 7LH
Tel: 01452 740260

(Stroudwater Canal)

This welcoming pub proudly proclaims itself to be a canalside inn, and its situation is as good as any on a navigable canal. A log fire, real ales (many from local breweries), and imaginative food make it a very inviting place to spend an evening – and accommodation is available.

SHIP INN

Brimscombe, Gloucestershire

Brimscombe Hill, Brimscombe Port,
Stroud, Gloucestershire
Tel: 01453 884388

Brimscombe Port was once a 'transhipment' port where Severn trows would unload their cargoes into Thames barges, for the rest of the journey across the Cotswolds. It will surely once again become a busy port when the ever-industrious Cotswold Canals Trust's work is done, but for now, there are a few reminders of the canal that once ran here, and the Ship Inn is one. Real ale and cider.

DANEWAY INN

Sapperton, Gloucestershire

Sapperton, Gloucestershire
GL7 6LN
Tel: 01285 760297
www.thedaneway.com

(Thames & Severn Canal)

Just a few yards from the western portal of Sapperton Tunnel, a real, stone-built Cotswolds pub that has miraculously escaped being gentrified. Its beers and ciders (Wadworths and Westons) are perfectly kept, its bacon butties and ham and eggs delicious. Camping is available and there's a music festival.

TUNNEL HOUSE INN *(Thames & Severn Canal)*

Coates, Gloucestershire

Coates, Cirencester,
Gloucestershire GL7 6PW
Tel: 01285 770280
www.tunnelhouse.com

At the eastern portal of Sapperton Tunnel, and a favourite with well-to-do students from the nearby Royal Agricultural College – but nonetheless welcoming and interesting in equal measure. Fixtures and fittings are idiosyncratic (a dentist's chair?) and, endearingly, a few tables are kept reservation-free, so locals can always find a place. Happily, brown signs now make the Tunnel House, once famously elusive to the driver, easy to locate.

LLANGOLLEN CANAL
AND MONTGOMERY CANAL

Hurleston to Llangollen: 44 miles/21 locks/3 tunnels
Montgomery Canal, Frankton Junction to Newtown: 35 miles/25 locks

The overwhelming popularity of the Llangollen Canal never seems to waver – and why should it, for this is a truly magnificent canal, from its quiet beginnings in the dairylands of Cheshire through to its fantastic climax in the dramatic mountains of North Wales. But there is a price to pay for all this scenic grandeur, as the Llangollen suffers from severe overcrowding in high summer – an out of season visit is strongly recommended. Leaving the Shropshire Union Canal at Hurleston Junction, the waterway slips quietly through a timeless landscape of black and white cows and black and white houses. The pretty villages of Wrenbury and Marbury serve to enhance the rural idyll. By contrast, Grindley Brook locks are often the scene of frenzied activity in high season – the lockkeeper is normally on hand to offer expert guidance to inexperienced boat crews.

The mountains of Wales, initially just grey/blue smudges on the western horizon, are coming ever closer now, but first there is Shropshire's very own Lake District to enjoy: a series of delightful meres grouped around the handsome town of Ellesmere. Passing Frankton Junction, where the Montgomery Canal heads off towards Newtown, you ascend the canal's final two locks at New Marton.

Dramatic aqueducts are like London buses hereabouts: you wait ages for one and then two come along together. First there's Chirk and then fabulous Pontcysyllte, where the canal crosses the River Dee on an incredible structure 1,000 feet long, 127 tall at its deepest point and comprising an iron trough supported by 18 stone pillars.

And then you're on the last lap into lovely Llangollen, a town made famous by its annual Eisteddfod. Horsedrawn trip boats operate on the final two-mile section up to Horseshoe Falls, although powered craft must turn at the last winding hole just beyond the Wharf.

Montgomery Canal
Closed in 1936 following a breach, the 'Monty' is slowly being restored to full navigation. Never less than pleasant, the canal has some beautiful reaches, notably in the vicinity of Berriew close to the current limit of navigation.

DUSTY MILLER

Wrenbury, Cheshire

The Llangollen Canal through Wrenbury boasts three attractive single-span timber bridges that are raised and lowered by counter-balancing beam weights. Next to No 20, on one side of the canal, is one of the bases for Alvechurch Boats and, on the other, is the Dusty Miller, now a pub but originally built as a corn mill in the late 1800s.

The present building is known as Sumner Mill and this is where the current licensee, Mark Sumner, comes in. Mark's great grandfather, Arthur, bought the mill and used it for storing animal feeds, potatoes and cheese. This produce was then sent by canal to Manchester market. Arthur even bought a couple of his own boats from the Shropshire Union Railway & Canal Company.

The mill was converted into a restaurant in about 1970, but was bought by

Robinson's Brewery of Stockport later that decade and turned into a pub. Mark was working in the pub trade and had always had a yearning to be a landlord in his uncle's old mill. So, when an opportunity arose in 1997, he, with the help of two other local men, took over the lease.

You go into a tiled bar area with stools, an oak settle and a refectory table. On the bar itself stands a small barrel of Old Tom, a staggering 8.5% winter beer. Customers are offered a taste before they buy and encouraged to partake of it in half pints only. There are photos of the old mill and of the canal and then, slightly incongruously, some pictures of racehorses. Apparently, in 1928, a locally-trained horse, Hollyhurst Tipperary Tim, had been taken by train from Wrenbury to Liverpool to compete in the Grand National. Only two horses finished out of a record field of 42, and he came in first at 100-1.

The pub opens out into an L-shape with windows overlooking the canal, while upstairs there is a restaurant, which has a more cosy, rustic feel with wooden floors, polished tables and candelabras. The history of the building resonates up here with evidence of the 'taking-in door' and crane support. Marks on the floor indicate an old, rather crude, stocktaking method: as a sack was taken away, a mark was made in its place. Outside, there are tables alongside the canal and in a lovely gravelled area behind the pub.

The Dusty Miller has an all-year round loyal clientele of food followers. And rightly so. The food here is delicious, most of it local produce or from the North West of England. It's English cooking at its best, whether you're having a snack, like chargrilled Cheshire smoked bacon with Bury black pudding, or dining in style upstairs on braised British beefsteak pie cooked in Old Tom. Mark, who is also the chef, has a penchant for cheese. There is always a cheese of the week alongside such delights as Creamy Lancashire and Shropshire Blue.

If you're travelling by boat, watch out for road rage from the motorists held up by the lift bridge – horns blowing, fists shaking – before you tie up for a visit to the Dusty Miller. And, if you are one of those motorists, calm down, drive across the bridge (after the boat has gone through, of course), turn into the car park and spend an hour or so savouring the delights of this classic, canalside pub. Unwind a little, but watch out for the Old Tom.

PUB FACTS

Location	Cholmondeley Road, Wrenbury, Cheshire CW5 8HG
Tel	01270 780537
Email	admin@dustymiller-wrenbury.com
Website	www.dustymiller-wrenbury.co.uk
Licensee/Chef	Mark Sumner
Opening hours	Mon–Sat 11am–3pm, 6.30pm–11pm, Sun 12pm–3pm, 7pm–10.30pm
Food served	Mon–Sat 12pm–2pm, 6.30pm–9.30pm, Sun 12pm–2pm, 7pm–9pm (No food on Mondays in winter) Starters £3.95–£5.75, Mains £9.95–£14.35
Real ales	Robinson's Unicorn, plus Robinson's seasonal beers, including Old Tom in the winter and Robin at Christmas
Moorings	Just beyond the pub on the towpath side

WILLEY MOOR LOCK TAVERN

near Whitchurch, Shropshire

PUB FACTS

Location	Tarporley Road, nr Whitchurch, Shropshire SY13 4HF
Tel	01948 663274
Website	www.willeymoorlock.co.uk
Proprietors	Elsie, Beverley and Graeme Gilkes
Opening hours	Mon–Sat 12pm–2.30pm (3pm in summer), 6pm–11pm, Sun 12pm–3pm, 7pm–10.30pm
Food served	Lunchtimes 12pm–2pm, evenings 6pm–9pm
Real ales	Theakston Bitter, and a variety of guest beers, including Abbeydale Moonshine, Hook Norton Best Bitter, Newby Wyke Sidewinder, Hoskins JHB
Moorings	Above the lock on the towpath side

The house alongside Willey Moor Lock on the Llangollen Canal was originally built as a lockkeeper's cottage in the late eighteenth century. It was sold as a private house in 1956. As pleasure traffic grew on the canal, it was converted into a restaurant in the 1970s, serving, according to an early edition of the *Waterways World* Guide to the Llangollen, "informal meals". Did that mean you didn't have to wear a tie? The Gilkes family turned it into a pub in 1981 and they are still running it today. Now it's mum, Elsie, with daughter, Beverley, and son, Graeme, as cellar man.

Although only a few hundred yards from the A49, it has a quiet, rural and isolated feel, particularly if you have arrived from Marbury or Grindley Brook by boat. The cottage has been extended on both sides, but the pub still has a cosy, intimate atmosphere: log fires, beams and low ceilings, with the usual harnesses and hunting prints on the walls but, more unusually, there are also teapots everywhere of all shapes, sizes and colours.

Outside, you can sit on the lockside and watch the many boats locking through and there is a fenced garden for children to play in. While I was there, a posse of novice boaters arrived in a hire boat from Wrenbury. As it was only their third lock of the trip, they were still a little puzzled and were delighted to receive a few tips on locking technique. The old stable block beside the lock is a very attractive listed building, which houses the wide variety of real ales, lovingly looked after by Graeme.

The food to go with the beer is no-nonsense pub grub, ranging from steaks and scampi to well-filled sandwiches and chips, of course, all at very reasonable prices. Bear in mind that the pub does not take credit cards.

The other way to arrive at Willey Moor Lock is on foot. The Sandstone Trail joins the towpath here. Originally opened in 1974, it has recently been extended and now covers 34 miles between Frodsham and Whitchurch. It starts near the River Weaver, crosses the Shroppie near to Wharton's Lock and the Shady Oak pub and, from Willey Moor Lock, it uses three miles of the towpath of the Llangollen through Grindley Brook. It follows the sandstone ridge and goes through delightful countryside.

As far as I know, willey is an Old English word meaning 'willow wood'. If you know any different, please let me know. Anyway, the Willey Moor Lock Tavern is what I call a proper pub: family run, friendly and unpretentious, with cracking beer, good food and a wonderful setting. What more could you want?

OTHER PUBS WORTH TRYING

*Llangollen Canal, Montgomery Canal and
Monmouthshire & Brecon Canal*

NAVIGATION *(Montgomery Canal)*

Maesbury Marsh , Oswestry

Maesbury Marsh, Oswestry,
Shropshire SY10 8JB
Tel: 01691 672958
www.thenavigation.co.uk

Maesbury Marsh is a textbook example of a
rural community looking to the 21st century
(their futuristic Post Office is a marvel), and
nowhere more than at the Navigation. Local,
ethically-reared meat, lovingly prepared, forms the
centrepiece of an imaginative menu; the beer is
up to scratch, and the resident Alsatian is friendly!
Visit at lunchtime, or between 6pm and 7pm, to
get top pub food for less.

QUEEN'S HEAD INN *(Montgomery Canal)*

West Felton, Oswestry

Queens Head, West Felton,
Oswestry, Shropshire SY11 4EB
Tel: 01691 610255

Situated just where the busy A5 to North Wales
crosses the Montgomery Canal., yet still with a
real canal feel to it. An excellent stop-off if you're
heading to Wales (it's child-friendly, too).

THE BRIDGEND INN *(Monmouthshire & Brecon)*

Govilon, Gwent

Church Lane, Govilon, Abergavenny,
Gwent NP7 9RP
Tel: 01873 830177

A pub enthusiast could spend a very happy week's
boating holiday on the isolated Mon & Brec, and
this is one of the stand-out pubs. An excellent
reputation for its beer, with live music on Fridays.
Moor up nearby and work up an appetite with a
walk in the Brecon Beacons!

STAR INN *(Monmouthshire & Brecon)*

Talybont-on Usk, Powys

Talybont-on-Usk, Powys LD3 7YX
Tel: 01874 676635

Just what a real pub should be. At long tables in the
front bar, you'll rub shoulders with walkers from
the Beacons, cyclists on the Taff Trail, and regulars
in for their favourite beer – and good beer it is,
too (real cider also available). No-nonsense food,
such as a rich steak and ale pie, is complemented
by more creative specials. The pub has a close
connection with the canal – perhaps too close, as
photos of a canal breach into the bar show!

THE BROADS AND EAST ANGLIA

The Broads is the accepted term for the self-contained navigational area based on five rivers: the Ant, Bure, Thurne, Waveney and Yare, plus various branches and the Broads themselves. These are a series of shallow lakes, many thought to have resulted from 13th and 14th century peat extraction.

The northern rivers (Ant, Bure and Thurne) are by far the busiest. But even here there are plenty of places to escape the crowds. To cruise (or, even better, sail) gently across Hickling Broad on a warm summer's evening is a memorable experience. Horsey Mere and Martham Broad are similarly remote outposts, and from the latter it is an enjoyable walk to the beach at Winterton.

To cross from the Northern Broads to the Southern requires passage across Breydon Water, an invigorating voyage that requires care and attention to avoid stranding at low water. The southern rivers are perhaps the most rewarding, the Waveney and the Yare being prettier than their northern counterparts. Finally, don't miss the last few navigable miles of the Waveney up to Geldeston, a sleepily picturesque village that perfectly epitomises the lesser known Broads.

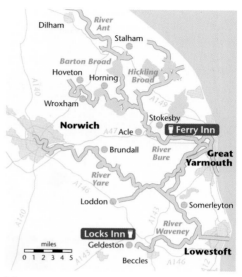

Nene
The Nene is an astonishingly lovely river, and unspoilt and uncrowded too as it makes its way through lush countryside between Northampton and Peterborough.

Great Ouse
The Great Ouse and tributaries have a fantastic variety of scenery and pass through a host of delightful towns and villages – as well as the beautiful university city of Cambridge.

THE FERRY INN

Stokesby, Norfolk

PUB FACTS

Location	Stokesby, Norfolk NR29 3EX
Tel	01493 751096
Lessee	Tracey Bean
Opening hours	Easter–October 11am–11pm Winter Mon–Fri 12pm – 2.30pm, 5.30pm–11pm, Sat & Sun 11am – 11pm
Food served	Mon–Sat 11.30am–2.30pm, 6pm–9pm, Sun 12pm–3pm, 6pm–9pm
Real ales	Adnams Beers – Bitter, Broadside & Explorer (summer only) plus a guest beer
Moorings	Outside the pub (phone ahead and reserve), public moorings by the park, & privately-owned moorings (£5) just beyond the pub

"I like everything about living here. I can look out of the window and no matter what the weather's doing, for me it's wonderful. Amazing light and fantastic views." These are the words of one of Norfolk's youngest landladies (the youngest when she started running a pub at 22 years old).

Norfolk is a staggering place to visit, made all the more interesting by the rivers and lakes which make up the fascinating navigation known as the Norfolk & Suffolk Broads. The rivers are the Yare, Bure, Ant, Thurne and Waveney and the lakes were originally peat workings dating from the thirteenth century.

The River Bure is navigable for thirty miles from Coltishall to Great Yarmouth. Nine and a half miles from Yarmouth is the little riverside village of

Stokesby. During the 19th century, Stokesby was a thriving place. There were carpenter, wheelwright and blacksmith's shops and a windmill grinding wheat for flour. There was a pork butcher's, a general store, a dressmaker, shoemaker, bricklayer and brazier. The Ferry Inn was the hub of the village. From the nearby staithe, a ferry carried people and goods across the river. The journey taken by this square, flat-bottomed boat, which was winched across, meant it was only two miles to the village of Acle, instead of eight by the old road.

The pub had a large barn for storing farm produce and there was a smaller brick building alongside the staithe for the storage of goods in transit, like coal. Wherries, the local sailing craft with their large single sails, called here regularly to load and unload their cargoes.

But, in 1910, the local squire decided to build a new road to Acle and, within a few years, the ferry had ceased to operate.

Today, you may wave in vain from the Acle side of the river for someone to pick you up. So, make sure you either arrive on the north side of the river or, better still, come by boat. You'll find that the staithe and its little brick building are still there, and the beautiful barn, but even better news for the hungry and thirsty is that the pub is still going strong.

The Ferry Inn has a lovely atmosphere. There is a large bar adorned with brasses and pictures of wherries, a rustic restaurant, and a pool and darts room. In the summer months, the riverside garden buzzes with the chatter of boaters who have called in for refreshment. In the winter, the fire blazes and the locals hunker down and talk about the weather or play for the various darts, pool and quiz teams.

There's always good food available, much of it home cooked. This all has to be washed down by some of the finest beer in the country made by Adnams at its superb brewery in Southwold. Tracey also prides herself on her wine list. *Chacun à son goût!*

THE LOCKS INN

Geldeston, Norfolk

PUB FACTS

Location	Locks Lane, Geldeston, Norfolk NR34 OHW
Tel	01508 518414
Website	www.geldestonlocks.co.uk
Managers	Colin & Teresa Smith
Opening hours	Week before Easter–October: 12pm–close (no later than 12.30am weekdays, 1am Fri/Sat), Winter: 5pm–11.30pm (Wed/ Thu), 12pm–12.30am (Fri–Sun)
Food served	12pm–2.30pm, 6pm–8.30pm (no food Sun eve)
Real ales	Beers from Green Jack Brewery plus guests
Moorings	24 hour free moorings adjacent to pub

The River Waveney used to be navigable from the confluence of the Yare at Breydon Water for 30 miles to Bungay. Now the head of navigation is at the site of Geldeston Locks, a remote spot in the middle of the marshes. There's little of the lock structures to see now but, for hundreds of years until 1934, wherries carried raw materials in and beer out from the thriving brewing and malting industries in Bungay.

A cottage was built by the locks in the 1560s for the mill-keeper. It was subsequently occupied by the lock-keeper. In the mid-17th century, it was licensed as a public house.

The river marks the border between Norfolk and Suffolk and the pub provided a haven for cross border smuggling and illegal prize fighting.

The 20th century marked the period of several long-standing publicans. In 2004 the pub was bought by the Green Jack Brewery. It is a remarkable place, probably one of the remotest pubs in England. If you don't arrive by water, either on your own or on a hired boat or on the Big Dog Ferry, which travels regularly from Beccles every day in the summer, you either have to walk across the marshes or drive from Geldeston village half a mile down a track.

The original building still stands and is the main bar of the pub. It has a flag stoned floor, an open fire, a piano, hops and agricultural implements hanging everywhere and, at night, is lit by gas mantles and candles. Outside, there is a huge riverside garden.

You go to the Locks Inn for many reasons: the setting, the friendliness of the staff, the atmosphere, the food and the beer. The beer is brewed by Green Jack Brewery and wonderful it is. Try any of them. The most popular is Orange Wheat Beer that has citrus and marmalade flavours. I loved the flowery, hoppy Canary, but there's also Grasshopper, a dark copper-coloured bitter and Gone Fishing (which is used to make the batter for the pub's famous haddock), a strong golden pale ale. You need to keep going back because there's Rumcask Cider to sample

(which has been stored in old rum barrels) or a guest ale from the many Waveney Valley independent breweries.

And there's the food. Apart from the haddock, there are delightful home-made pies like steak & Grasshopper Ale, shepherd's and chicken and leek. But the most popular night is Friday. That's 'Curries of the World Night'. All prepared from scratch by Colin, on one evening there may be curries from Thailand, Jamaica, Sumatra and India.

You never quite know what to expect. You might walk into a family party, a bunch of folk musicians doing their stuff or Old Glory, a local Molly troupe, with their blackened faces, dancing away and pushing their coin-boxes at you. There might be over 200 people on the lawn on a hot, sunny day or a few hardy souls gathered round the fire on a winter's night.

Colin says it's wonderful in winter: "We love it. It's magical. The proverbial Norfolk lazy wind goes straight through you, but push open the door of the pub and there's a buzz of music with violins and guitars going, the fire's roaring and the candles are glimmering."

OTHER PUBS WORTH TRYING

The Broads and East Anglia

KINGS HEAD

Wadenhoe, Northamptonshire
Church Street, Wadenhoe PE8 5ST
Tel: 01832 720024
www.kingsheadwadenhoe.co.uk

(River Nene)

Popular with walkers, cyclists and boaters, the King's Head lies on a lovely section of the Nene. There is a pleasant garden, a large grassy paddock and a welcoming interior. A fine selection of real ales and good food are served daily.

HAYCOCK INN

Wansford, Cambridgeshire
The Haycock Hotel, London Road,
Wansford, Peterborough PE8 6JE
Tel: 01780 782223
www.thehaycock.co.uk

(River Nene)

Dating from 1620, an historic coaching inn on an idyllic, tree-lined reach of the River Nene. Famous guests – Mary Queen of Scots, Diana, Princess of Wales – have called here, but present-day boaters are assured of a warm welcome too. A fine selection of beers, wines and spirits and superb food.

FIVE MILES INN

Upware, Cambridgeshire
Old School Lane, Upware,
Cambridgeshire CB7 5ZR
Tel: 01353 721654
Opening hours: every day 12pm–12am

(River Cam)

Remote fenland surrounds this much refurbished inn at Upware on the Cam, also known as 'Five miles from anywhere, no hurry.' Plentiful moorings, attractive gardens, a spacious riverside lounge and a fine restaurant make this a popular venue.

CUTTER INN

Ely, Cambridgeshire
42 Annesdale, Ely,
Cambridgeshire CB7 4BN
Tel: 01353 662713

(Great Ouse)

An enviable location right on the waterside. Fully refurbished in 2006, there are log fires in winter and wonderful sunsets from the terrace in summer. Real ale drinkers are well-catered for and full meals and bar snacks are served daily.

OLD FERRY BOAT INN *(Great Ouse)*

Holywell, Cambridgeshire
Back Lane, Holywell, St Ives,
Cambridgeshire PE27 4TG
Tel: 01480 463227
www.oldferryboat.com

Thought by many to be England's oldest inn, this is a pure delight, with white stone walls, thatched roof and lovely garden overlooking the broad waters of the Great Ouse. A good range of beers are on offer and food is served lunchtimes and evenings; there's accommodation too.

FOSSDYKE CANAL & RIVER WITHAM

Torksey to Boston: 43 miles/3 locks
Witham Navigable Drains: 42 miles/2 locks

The Fossdyke Canal runs from the River Trent at Torksey through somewhat flat, featureless scenery to Lincoln, from where the River Witham is navigable to Boston and thus the Wash. The Witham Navigable Drains offer a further 40 or so miles of navigable waterways traversing an archetypal – and eerily remote – Fenland landscape.

The principal appeal of these waters lies in their astonishingly remote nature: away from the madding crowd, etc.

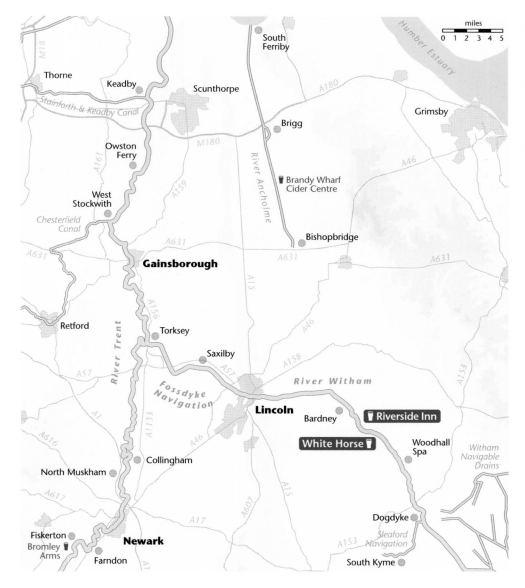

THE RIVERSIDE INN

Southrey, Lincolnshire

PUB FACTS

Location	Ferry Road, Southrey, Lincolnshire LN3 5TA
Tel	01526 398374
Email	theriversideinn@btinternet.com
Proprietor	Nathan Beacon
Opening hours	11am–11pm
Food served	12pm–3pm, 6.30pm–9pm
Real ales	Tom Wood's Best Bitter and Bomber County, plus two guest beers
Moorings	River bank, 50 yards from pub

If you've ever boated along the River Witham in Lincolnshire, you won't need me to tell you how straight it is. There are compensations: the river's deep and the vast skies are always entrancing, but the banks are high and there are few bends to test your boating skills and only one lock at Bardney. If you are travelling towards Boston, you will see the 'Boston Stump', the tower of St Botolph's Church, for many miles before you reach this fascinating town. In fact, for quite a while, it doesn't seem to be getting any closer.

All the more reason to tie up and discover the delights of some of the riverside pubs. At Southrey, pull up on the north bank and visit the Riverside Inn. There is a small landing stage available.

The pub is a few strides away across what once was a railway line.

And that's the reason the pub is where it is. It was built in 1896 as the Railway Hotel to service the passengers on the Lincoln to Boston Railway, which had opened in 1848. It had seven bedrooms! Who would have stayed at such a remote place? Well, it was very popular with fishermen, who would have travelled from Lincoln or Boston to spend a day or two trying their angling luck on the banks of the river.

The railway line was closed down in 1969, one more of Mr Beeching's executions, his savage attempt to rationalise our railway system. Most of the anglers drifted away and the pub had to try and survive by attracting boaters and motorists in search of something different.

Now called the Riverside Inn, it has a lovely garden, and a feeling of remoteness. They serve local Tom Wood's traditional ales from the Highwood Brewery. The Best Bitter is deliciously hoppy and the Bomber County, at 4.8%, is more intense and malty. Drink these with some of the traditional delicious home-cooked food. It's all locally

sourced – the meat from Lincoln, the fish from Grimsby and the veg from Hemswell. The menu carries the Tastes of Lincoln approved logo.

The pub is obviously much quieter in the winter. The locals drink there and play in the dominoes team, but Southrey only has a population of 200, so people need to be encouraged to visit from farther afield. The old railway track has become part of the Sustrans' Water Rail Way from Lincoln to Boston. If you haven't got a boat, get out the bike and visit the Riverside Inn.

WHITE HORSE INN

Metheringham, Lincolnshire

PUB FACTS

Location	Dunston Fen, Metheringham, Lincolnshire LN4 3AP
Tel	01526 398341
Email	info@whitehorseinn.biz
Website	www.whitehorseinn.biz
Proprietors	The Stout family
Opening hours	Mon–Fri 12pm–3pm, 7pm–11pm, Sat 12pm–12am, Sun 12pm–11pm (Closed first two weeks of Jan & Mon lunchtimes Jan & Feb)
Food served	Tue–Fri 12pm–2.30pm, 7pm–9pm, Sat/Sun 12pm–9pm. Bank Holiday Mondays (then no food Tue)
Real ales	A selection of three guest ales from eg. Poachers Brewery, Newby Wyke Brewery and Cottage Brewery
Moorings	Outside pub and on towpath opposite

No-one seems quite sure when the White Horse was built but the original building was probably erected in the late nineteenth century. There is a black and white photo in the pub taken in 1906. It was then called the White Horse Hotel and there were two ferries, one for people and one for carts and cattle. Another photo taken in 1964 shows one ferry looking exceedingly worse for wear. The vicar is on board, presumably praying for a safe crossing for the people from Dunston going to catch the train at Southrey Station. In the early 1980s, it was hauled on to the bank and declared unsafe.

The pub has been completely rebuilt since the 1960s photo. It has a large extension at the front, built to feed fishing parties, which frequented the pub until something happened to the fish and they and the fishermen went away. This room is now a pleasantly decorated 60-

seater dining room. There is a large bar area with a wood-burning stove and, outside, a lovely garden and, in the summer months, a marquee with patio heaters. This is where the annual August Bank Holiday Beer Festival is held, when people come from all around to sample 25 different brews.

There are always good local beers available and the pub also has a reputation for its home cooked food. From the main menu, try spicy crab cakes (£3.75), Chicken Kiev (£6.95) and bangers and mash with Lincolnshire sausages (£6.75) or go for the bargain steak for two (£23.95 including a bottle of house wine). There are specials every day, like fish pie or steak in Guinness and, on Sunday, a roast costs you £5.95 (it's best to book for this).

The pub is very much family run by James and Louisa and mum, Jacky, and is very 'hands on'. They only took over in 2006 but they love the life and revel in the peace and quiet of the fens and the river. They were snowed in, or so they thought, on their first Christmas

but found brave or foolhardy customers turning up, testing out the capabilities of their 4x4s. People come from the surrounding villages, from the adjoining caravan park and, of course, by boat (the easiest route). Overnight mooring is free as long as you use the pub. And why wouldn't you? Even the fishermen are returning, and you might be in the bar to hear one of their incredible stories, or some of the older customers telling you of how they learnt to swim in the river while staying at the pub, or the days when there were goats and chickens in the bar.

The River Witham has been navigable since Roman times but was improved in the eighteenth and early nineteenth centuries. There was much commercial traffic on it until the end of the 1st World War. Since then, it has remained as a rural refuge for pleasure boats, for those people seeking quieter waters. Please keep using it and, while you're at it, enjoy a pint and a meal at this most welcoming of pubs.

OTHER PUBS WORTH TRYING

River Witham and the Trent and Humber waterways

BROMLEY ARMS *(River Trent)*

Fiskerton, Nottinghamshire

Main Street, Fiskerton,
Nottinghamshire NG25 0UL
Tel: 01636 830789

Good views of the river characterise this welcoming pub by the Trent and the terrace seating area is popular on warm sunny days. It can be crowded with walkers at weekends – rucksacks everywhere! There's a wide choice of beers and good value bar meals are served lunchtimes and evenings.

BRANDY WHARF CIDER CENTRE *(River Ancholme)*

Brandy Wharf, Lincolnshire

Brandy Wharf, Lincolnshire DN21 4RU
Tel: 01652 678364

Quite unique, this back-of-beyond pub in deepest rural Lincolnshire has one of the country's best range of ciders; some on tap, some bottled. There's a lovely picnic area too, in an apple orchard no less. A wonderful day out for the cider enthusiast.

County Index

149

PUB NAME INDEX